■□■□ Black Dog Publishing
Architecture Art Design Fashion History
Photography Theory and Things

FORM FOLLOWS IDEA
AN INTRODUCTION TO DESIGN POETICS

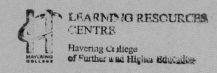
Maxine Naylor
Ralph Ball

foreword

Jeremy Myerson

Not for nothing are Maxine Naylor and Ralph Ball widely regarded as among Britain's most thoughtful furniture designers. They have been building up to this book for a long time, slowly and carefully generating the intellectual impetus to carry their study of the meaning of objects into the territory where design meets art. Practical philosophy could be one way to describe their approach.

The significance of *Form Follows Idea* lies not so much in the body of work itself, however much you admire the creativity of the individual pieces, but in the resonant ideas that underpin them. One of the fundamental notions in *Form Follows Idea* is the idea that design itself can be a critical medium for cultural reflection without recourse to interpretation by the design critic who writes about the artefact.

In a world of increasingly strident contextual debate about design, in which the narrative is mainly generated and sustained by external commentators, Naylor and Ball reclaim the role for practising designers. They do this by embedding the narrative in the object itself: chairs and lights, for example, go beyond their function or even their symbolism to playfully reflect on a cultural meaning. You don't

develop this strategy overnight. Naylor and Ball have been edging this way gradually, using their fascination with the Modern Movement to question in a gentle, enigmatic but ultimately confrontational way what modern design really means.

The absolute values of Modernism are so well defined and clearly understood that Naylor and Ball have a fixed point in a turning world from which to conduct their elegant and ironic experiments with form, colour and texture. Modern design is thus celebrated in a critical way with such principles as honesty in materials and the avoidance of decoration subjected to the Postmodern twist.

Interestingly, in staking a claim for designers to control an alternative narrative of the object, Naylor and Ball don't approach their subject as a purely visual medium. Many of their ideas seem to emerge not through sketching but through language and wordplay as if they are literally taking the argument about Modernism at its word and turning it on its head.

There is a real relish for the lexicon that make the fusion of text and image in *Form Follows Idea* both unusual and adventurous. Words are described by

Naylor and Ball as "delicious, powerful and tenacious". Commentary and creative process are ambitiously intertwined so that the familiar character witnesses for the Modern Movement – Adolph Loos, Robert Venturi, Walter Gropius, Charles Eames and so on – are referenced not just in the text but in the pieces themselves.

Famous quotes are also deployed with intent to advance the critique. Laurie Anderson's memorable saying, "Writing about music is like dancing about architecture", is there to remind us what a risky strategy this can be. But it is almost as if Naylor and Ball are saying that if designers have lost their place in the critical debate about objects because of a lack of facility with words, then they can use language as a playful weapon to reclaim it.

These pages then contain a manifesto for a 'third way' in design, a championing of cultural enquiry within the object which goes beyond the idea that designers just design and the context of what they create must be defined and directed by others. Naylor and Ball's furniture and lighting is raw material for debate, angled towards artistic speculation rather than design for production, but they are unapologetic about that.

Form Follows Idea challenges not only the Modernist dictum of "form follows function" but more contemporary notions of design such as problem solving or commercial branding by refracting Modernist design principles through the artist's eye. Ralph Ball says he originally came to furniture from an interest in sculpture and painting because he wanted to create practical work. Now the very expressiveness of his chosen medium has taken him full circle back to his artistic roots.

The central elements of Ralph Ball's work, delicate aesthetics combined with rigorous engineering, were evident early in his career. He had already studied at colleges of art in Hull and Leeds, freelanced in interior design and worked in the office furniture industry during the 1970s, when he first came to national prominence with his Royal College of Art (RCA) degree show in 1980.

Ball's Aero light and sheet steel shelving suspended on wires at the RCA brought him into the orbit of architect Norman Foster. Between 1981 and 1984, he was part of the team which developed influential furniture designs for Foster's own office and Foster's landmark Renault building in Swindon.

In 1985 Ball formed a design partnership with his professional and personal partner Maxine Naylor, a graduate of Middlesex and Buckinghamshire College, which is right in the cradle of the furniture industry. By this time Naylor had already established an independent reputation as an experimental designer-maker, exploring the potential of lighting with tension wires and pvc sheet, and together they began to challenge the borders between art, craft and design.

That same year, Ball resumed his relationship with the Royal College of Art as a visiting lecturer, uniquely going on to work in three separate RCA departments – furniture, industrial design and jewellery – over the next decade. Maxine Naylor also tutored at the RCA from the late 80s, going on to become course leader in furniture design.

Today Ralph Ball is Professor of design at Central Saint Martins University of the Arts, London, and Maxine Naylor is Professor of Design at the University of Lincoln. As their reputations have grown in academic and design circles, so too has the general clamour to establish proper definitions for design research. With *Form Follows Idea* Naylor

and Ball identify themselves as key players in this debate, their experimentation through design making a significant contribution to the research field.

One of America's leading thinkers in this area, Stephen Wilcox of Design Science in Philadelphia, has described how design research grew out of three basic types of research. The first is ethnography, an observational approach derived from anthropology and folklore; the second is scholarship, with its focus on checking multiple sources derived from history and journalism; and the third is experimentation, with an emphasis on making and presenting models and prototypes derived from psychology, physics and other sciences. All research depends on conjecture and refutation, says Wilcox, and the crucial issue is validity.

The conjecture is the creative part and designers are very good at that. But then researchers must do their best to refute their own ideas. This is where many designers fall down, lacking the in-built scepticism to challenge their own speculations. Maxine Naylor and Ralph Ball do not suffer from this syndrome. Taking experimentation as their main design research method, they subject their ideas to a critical process of refutation, always questioning the work and using a scholarly approach to the milestones of Modernism to enhance its depth.

One could describe this approach as somewhat introspective – Ball knows this and once staged an exhibition called Introspective Furniture – but it is also full of insight and engagement. *Form Follows Idea* captures two exceptional practitioner/researchers in their prime.

Jeremy Myerson is Professor of Design Studies and co-director of the Helen Hamlyn Research Centre at the Royal College of Art.

introduction

The chief enemy of creativity is 'good' sense.

Pablo Picasso

Form in relation to design can be expressed in many diverse ways and involves a vast array of materials, textures and colours; also issues of shape, scale, proportion and weight, and not least cultural associations in relation to function, need and desire and to meaning, value and context.

Form follows Idea represents the most recent in a series of ongoing investigations that we have conducted through our design work into different ways of representing form. In each of these investigations a different word was inserted after 'form follows_____' in order to explore and develop a formal, visual vocabulary via different frames of reference and focus. It can be correctly assumed here that 'form follows geometry' produced a different and more abstract body of work in contrast to that explored via 'form follows value'. The same diversity is true for other positions explored in the 'form follows_____' investigations and provides a rich and rounded formal vocabulary.

Form follows Idea is the most open ended of all of these investigations and is the first to be documented in book form. It is one where no preliminary guidelines have been defined in advance. Design is always more complex than any set of rules can encompass and

Chinese Acrobat
The chair in side view is a clear visual expression of an asymmetrical object; something not equally balanced. The chair is often used in balancing acts, balanced on hand or head or balanced upon. Its visual asymmetry makes the chair a perfect choice for exaggerating the theatrical dynamics of the balancing act. The chairs' visual character makes the trick appear even more precarious.

Neil Dawson, Flying Chairs, 1993
The chairs here are in outline not fully formed but latent – an idea and a potential. Chairs do grow on trees, are one of the fruits of trees.

this book attempts to illustrate an activity we call 'poetic' design where all of the usual rules are thrown away in order to find new ones framed in a conceptual context.

Form follows Idea questions some of the established orthodoxy and protocols of design method – the diversion and limitation of the conventional uses of words, methods and systems.

Form follows idea or does idea follow form? The answer is that the two positions are inextricably linked and things are, of course, always more complicated and interesting than any axiom can hope to deliver definitively.

There is only one axiom that can be absolutely relied on: "absolutes, they come and they go". In this book then, ideas are up for visual examination and we are being rhetorical about rhetorical axioms. "Form follows idea" is a play on Louis Sullivan's most famous axiom "form follows function" and starts a process of inverting other famous axioms of Modernism for the untapped possibilities they might reveal when turned upside down.

Jerry N Uelsmann, Untitled, 2001
Latent narratives are present here. A
meeting has or is about to take place
or are the chairs meeting on their
own? Why has one chair fallen over
and what is that on the horizon?
The fallen chair is opposite to the
presence on the horizon: is there a
connection? Chairs have direction;
have fronts and backs. The seat when
unoccupied represents the absent
trace of a sitters shape and stands in
as a surrogate person.

In the world of the plastic arts it is a truism that actions, not axioms, speak louder than words. Axioms cannot save you; it is all in the visual telling. Stories in form are what this book is all about. Successful navigation between idea and form is all in the visual translation and narration and this is embodied in drawing, image and form making. In turn this means being visually articulate and requires a mature control of the translating medium. A weak idea cannot be rescued for long by superficial or flamboyant dressing and, similarly, a strong one can easily be lost through careless manifestation.

As this is about ideas articulated visually it is important to assert from the start that the visual material is the important part of this book, a reversal of the academic tradition where image is used to support and evidence a literary argument. In that genre images are mostly used as consolidators rather than containers of ideas. Here image and form are their own evidence and argument. Each image is its own self-contained story, each its own poetic substance and visual dialogue. This written text should be seen as a background, which underlines the images in a general way. Occasionally the image and text touch more specifically, all of the images, however are perfectly able to speak for themselves.

In addition, there is no specific agenda as to how this will all come out, but then that is part of the idea (and the poetics) of this book. *Form Follows Idea* records and reports an open process, which is in part determined by looking for, and responding to, form as it presents itself and using this both as a generator and container of ideas. The journey variously involves poetics, rhetoric and paradox and in this context the book's text and imagery reserves the right to be lyrical, emphatic and contradictory by turns and to produce objects which go beyond just 'another product'. The results are ideas, delivered in forms that ask questions, tell stories and comment on the culture of design.

This open process is one starting with few rules, which finds the rules as it goes along: a process declaring that intuition and 'post rationalisation' are entirely reasonable procedures, that are tested and proved in results. These methods are fully legitimate tools in the creative process but are often not declared (especially in design), precisely because they lack conventional rationality. Contrary to normal design practice the central driving idea here

Stacking chairs – orderly and rational.

A Triennale Series 7, Arne Jacobsen
B Boman Chair, Carl Boman
C GF 40/4, David Rowland
D DSS, Charles Eames
E Landi, Hans Coray
F Polyprop, Robin Day
G 4860, Joe Colombo
H Selene, Vico Magistretti
I Panton Chair, Verner Panton

stack of one

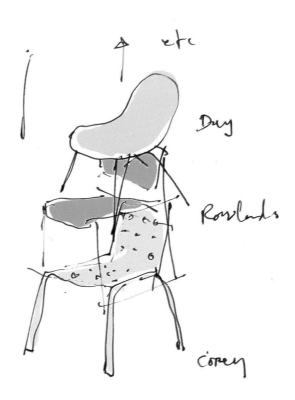

↑ etc

Day

Rowlands

Corey

Short stack
Incomplete history of stacking
a stack of one   chairs

Bell 2003

Michael Wolf
This provisional repair was probably pragmatic and unconscious. However, the poetic 'rightness' of a broken chair being returned to functional use by connecting it to a tree, the source of its being, is deliciously lyrical.

is to explore and illustrate a design position, which is not driven by problem solving, by commercial design concerns or by branding strategies. It is an activity of finding ideas and connections by playing with the cultural and formal components of objects; of finding and thinking through doing.

The book resists any form of prescribed, objective procedure. It attempts to expose myths about formal methodologies, revealing through practice not another formal method but a position: an attitude of mind. Form follows Idea represents a philosophical approach that is apparently contradictory: one that could be described as accidental and controlled, arbitrary and rigorous. It is not so much a theory as a frame of reference for questioning the nature and production of design delivery.

For example the title of this book and the image for the book cover came together as an intuitive combination rather than a strictly rational one. They were selected from a range of our own material laid out on the table. Independently considered they just look and sound right. Everybody involved liked the image, everybody liked the title, but do they fit together? The image clearly shows famous chairs, and this wasn't going to be just another book about

classic chairs. However, in this image, which is called Stack of One, the stacking chairs and the name simultaneously both do and don't quite stack up. This paradoxical visual commentary on function and form entirely suits the conceptual, visual position taken in the book. With a lack of precise fit but common intention, form follows idea, and function (stacking) is articulated in visual narrative rather than passing unnoticed. There will be more about this image later. The point to be made here, is that the words above and below this sentence were post-rationalised or consolidated, much later than the intuitive coming together of the image and the title for the book.

The irregular and irreverent image also activates an awkward correspondence with what might be termed orthodox design culture. There is, in the background, a latent imperative that design process should be orderly, tidy, and rational when the world plainly does not work like this. Yet a cultural nagging, ambient and constant, prevails; if only we could get all of our systems in place then everything will work and everything will be fine. Time spent managing the process has overtaken the creative activity of actually generating something. Filing is now more important than forming. This in turn reflects a

culture that lacks autonomous self-confidence and a willingness to trust in risk. A culture increasingly defined by rule serving and form filling accountancy rather than rule questioning. Organising is a preparatory and retrospective process not a generative one. It is useful when consolidating that which, in general, has already been proved to work, but it does not function well as a device for the generation of new ideas.

Form follows Idea presents an activity that is governed by responding with ideas and forms to ideas and forms. The response, in particular, is to ideas and forms, that often have a kind of establishment; a consolidated integrity, an orthodoxy conferred by time and survival: to everyday, ordinary, familiar and well-known things.

In looking for, and responding to, form as it presents itself and using this both as a generator and consolidator of ideas, Form follows Idea finds and responds to everyday, unwanted chairs among other things. It looks at them not in terms of individual, idiosyncratic forms but as general types, as categories of visual information. So, in this instance the book is in part about 'chair as idea'; chair as narrative idea. It is about design ideas and objects

This is an example of post-rationalisation, or post-consolidation, at work and of things falling together after they have been started. This image had been made and forgotten long before the line about "books high enough to sit on" had been written. The publisher, on an early draft reading, was unsure of the tone of this line yet it stayed in the text provisionally because we were, for no logical reason reluctant to lose it. Then this image re-emerged to reveal from where the text had been unconsciously extrapolated. This construction had been a quick, three-dimensional sketch made and photographed as a reminder to develop a chair along this conceptual line. It followed from some earlier work concerning the relationship of books to objects. The printed image revealed another coincidence entirely accidental but totally appropriate in its visual correspondence. The colours of the elements that made up the trolley were the same as those on the image of the chair on the top book of the pile. The book with that particular chair image was deliberately on the top of the pile because of its iconic status and diagrammatic quality – a chair of flat panels formally similar to the flat panels of books. The colour of the trolley on the other hand was an accident, which could not have turned out better had it been planned.

CHART SHOWING YARDAGE REQUIRED ON ALL DIFFERENT TYPES OF FURNITURE WITH REASONABLE ALLOWANCE FOR MATCHING

1. 5 YDS	2. 34 YDS	3. 6' 10 YDS / 7' 11 YDS / 9' 13 YDS	4. 6' 10 YDS / 7' 11 YDS / 9' 13 YDS	5. 6' 10 YDS / 7' 11 YDS / 9' 13 YDS	6. 6' 12 YDS / 7' 14 YDS / 9' 18 YDS
7. 14 YDS	8. 14 YDS	9. 11 YDS	10. 11 YDS	11. 12 YDS	12. 10 YDS
13. 10 YDS	14. $2\frac{1}{2}$ YDS	15. 6 YDS	16. 6 YDS	17. 6' 16 YDS	18. 13 YDS
19. 3 YDS	20. $5\frac{1}{2}$ YDS	21. 5 YDS	22. $6\frac{1}{2}$ YDS	23. $5\frac{1}{2}$ YDS	24. 4 YDS
25. 6 YDS	26. 6 YDS	27. 4 YDS	28. 7 YDS	29. $2\frac{1}{2}$ YDS	30. 3 YDS
31. $7\frac{1}{2}$ YDS	32. $2\frac{1}{2}$ YDS	33. 4 YDS	34. 7 YDS	35. 5 YDS	36. 5 YDS
37. $6\frac{1}{2}$ YDS	38. 5 YDS	39. 8 YDS	40. 4 YDS	41. 5 YDS	42. $4\frac{1}{2}$ YDS
43. 7 YDS	44. $3\frac{1}{2}$ YDS	45. 6 YDS	46. 6 YDS	47. $6\frac{1}{2}$ YDS	48. $6\frac{1}{2}$ YDS
49. $2\frac{1}{2}$ YDS	50. $1\frac{1}{2}$ YDS	51. 5 YDS	52. $1\frac{1}{2}$ YDS	53. $1\frac{1}{2}$ YDS	54. $2\frac{1}{2}$ YDS
55. $1\frac{1}{2}$ YDS	56. $3\frac{1}{2}$ YDS	57. $4\frac{1}{2}$ YDS	58. $4\frac{1}{2}$ YDS	59. $4\frac{1}{2}$ YDS	60. $2\frac{1}{2}$ YDS

made in response to celebrating the ordinariness of chairs and what we call "the poetics of the everyday". Being everyday it is therefore not about the famous icons of the genre. There are already substantial piles of that type of chair book – high enough for whole departments of design historians to sit on. It is not about the royalty of chairdom but about its ordinary citizens and the view of the 'chair in the street' so to speak. It is about the type of chair that does not live in the Vitra Design Museum, the Museum of Modern Art or the Victoria & Albert Museum.

There are chairs representing every kind of sitting function and visual whim, every kind of manifestation: from the ostentatious to the rudimentary, from the lyrical and poetic to the witless and bland. Despite this prolific variety they all fall into types with common features and this book includes a visual exploration of some of those types and common denominators. Chairs here are explored as commentary on themselves and their essential nature. In this book the poetics of the everyday notices, explores, expresses and celebrates the whole extraordinary, ordinary business of chairs and chairness. What they are and what they do: chair as a narrative idea.

Andy Lock, from Orchard Park, 2003
Untitled, sunlight, empty room
Untitled, vinyl chairs
Created in a dispossessed apartment building, encountered during
a brief hiatus between occupancy and demolition, the appearance
of these crude facsimiles of domestic space is reminiscent of a
dream, suggestive of a fantasy-space wherein fragments of
furniture and the fall of light take on forms, which are at once
melancholy and disquieting.

The work that emerges from this 'finding and responding' process is playful and serious, rhetorical and optimistic, valuing, embracing and reinterpreting the positive attributes in that which we already have. Extracting new ideas from old forms and new forms from old ideas. It suggests that the best that we have already works fine and that when it needs replacing it needs replacing with itself or with some thing of equivalent status, new or old.

What we do not need and should not accept is replacement by formally, materially or conceptually inferior versions of the same thing. This inferior form of replenishment is, however, a significant phenomenon in the contemporary furniture world. Neo-Modern 'repro' is everywhere. Just turn to the advertisements funding the pages of any design magazine; look at most of the exhibits in the trade design exhibitions. You will generally see translations of that which you have seen before, but often these translations are devoid of any notable, contemporary interpretation.

This is where most furniture design activity (with many inventive exceptions, including the design groups Memphis in the 1970s, Droog in the 1990s, and individual designers like Robert Venturi, Marcel Wanders, Jurgen Bey, and Hella Jongerius, among others) still seems to be; caught in a narrowing cul-de-sac and bumping up against itself in pastiche and facsimile.

From roughly 1860 to 1960, from Michael Thonet to Pop, furniture evolved in a proliferating and kaleidoscopic array of material, technological, structural and production innovations, coupled with an emerging Modernist ideology. Much of the front line innovation provided by new materials and technology has now moved to the digital world, emerging in microchip driven electronic products and services. If, as is now the case, the furniture profession (again with many notable exceptions) lacks the original creative impetus of materials technology and Modernist ideology, it needs alternative creative drivers.

Furniture must find other forms of cultural expression, other ideas. It cannot simply repeat itself with poorer and poorer versions. More and more of the same stylistic manipulations simply produce an endless cycle of Neo-Modernism: a kind of Spartan decadence. Many items of contemporary furniture have become ritualised form without content; these newer forms have in some sense become detached

from their original generative idea. They are not born out of an original impulse to explore material, structure or culture. They have no desire to say something in a new way. Their newness is not genuinely new; that is, embodying a new idea of expression. Their newness is merely the superficial newness of being recently made. These 'new' pieces are mostly facsimiles, ghosts standing in as insubstantial substitutes for the ideas of previous generations. These older ideas may still be valid when represented by the original or a genuinely authentic copy, i.e. one where the materials and process used are identical in every detail to the original. However, when copied superficially they become uncreative, a delivery to formula. Form follows form!

If there are now fewer material and manufacturing problems to solve in the general arena of furniture and lighting design then we must find forms of expression where structure and material resolution are taken as given and the designed object as cultural information can be contemplated. Invention now lies more in reconnecting and building authentic, narrative layers of meaning back into objects that have lost meaningful significance, rationale and value under the shear proliferation of bad copies.

Today production belongs to everybody with a computer. Speed, quantity and the seductive power of production have become ends rather than means. Meaning disappears as method takes over.

It is important to re-establish visual contemplation and communication: to put the brakes on unreflective proliferation and superficial replication. It is time to provide critical, ironic and playful commentary on our condition and our cultures of consumption of both material and information.

It's time to play and to play seriously. It is time to put the poetry back into design.

'this way up'   'sunrise and sunset'   'dawn and dusk'   Ralph Ball 00

Two examples of lighting concepts exploring the relationship between 'sun', 'light', and 'position'.

The standard, generic lampshade reconfigured in terms of the up and down perceptions of the sun's movement in sunrise and sunset, and the half light of dawn and dusk.

Chris Toby, 1991
A more literal interpretation: sunrise to midday. The 'sun' is mounted on a counterweighted beam with a dimmer switch set at the fulcrum. At horizontal the dimmer is off, rising and increasing in intensity until the vertical point of high noon is reached.

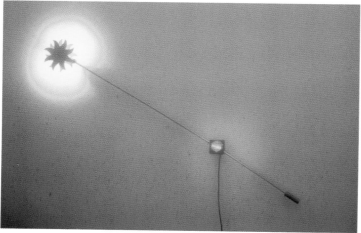

words and other things that get in the way

Writing about music is like dancing about architecture.

Laurie Anderson

words

Here is the first paradox. This is a book about a design process, which is sceptical regarding books about design process. Sceptical because when you get right down to it, writing is not designing. You don't do design by talking about it or writing it down. These activities are significant as starting points, generators and stimulators of certain kinds of speculation, reflection and revision but they are not the physical articulation. Words are delicious, powerful and tenacious. They are valuable, fabulously seductive and dangerously diversionary, all at the same time. They are so persuasive that they can conspire to convince many people that just talking and writing it down is the design process. Words allow us to live in our heads where we can always remain mentally pregnant with ideas; ideas are safe and protected in this deliciously speculative womb. Giving birth is a much more painful reality. Forcing the idea to live in the tactile, tangible, visual and visceral world is a demanding and genuinely creative exposure of a different kind and finally, is the only real test of a visual idea's true value.

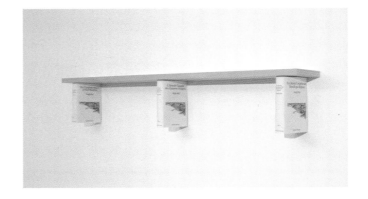

These two pieces are part of a collection of designs, which comment on the relationship between word and object, information and its storage.

The Complete History of Shelf Supports
Volumes of a multivolume work perform the function that the titles describe. The result is a visual pun in which the shelf is supported by the books instead of the other way around. The concept is taken further by the fact that the titles of the books indicate that the shelf is being supported not by mere books but by every type of shelf support that ever existed.

Coffee Table Book Table
The table takes its form and concept from the symbiotic relationship between design and books on design, which are often produced and consumed in greater numbers than the designed objects they illustrate. Here books made up of designed objects are themselves co-opted and subverted to become the contents of a designed object. The books are all copies of the International Design Yearbook built up year by year... each successive edition renders the previous one redundant in an inaccessible archive.

BLUE RED

It is undeniable that words and word play are tools that can be used in the development of creative ideas and forms; we use them all the time. Words are very important triggers but in the end words are not objects or images and explanations in words are poor substitutes for the real thing. Some information is beyond words: describe accurately, for example, the colour red. Art and design are image-based forms of articulation and it is through visual media that they must live and communicate.

Visual intelligence is no less a form of intelligence than verbal or literary intelligence. Literary intelligence however is dominant within our culture. Because of its dominance it insists with self-righteous and self appointed authority, that other forms of intelligence learn to communicate using its language and on its terms. However, artists and designers are visually-based thinkers and language is often not the most appropriate mode of communication for them.

In art and design education this practice of required literary translation has two questionable effects:

Firstly, it allows into the field of art and design more people than those who are genuinely visually literate. It allows people with limited visual intelligence to talk and write their way in; people who quickly learn to 'talk the talk' and to cushion and shore up insubstantial visual output with overly elaborate supportive text.

Second, it intimidates those with strong visual intelligence into feeling inadequate or disempowered because they cannot necessarily research and report as fluently and meaningfully in a medium, which is not as natural to them.

However, in reassurance to the visually literate, the following are offered:

Among the several sins that I have been accused of committing none is more false than the one that I have as the principal object of my work the spirit of research. When I paint my object is to show what I have found not what I am looking for. In art intentions are not sufficient and as we say in Spanish, love must be proved by facts and not by reasons.

Pablo Picasso

A true photograph need not be explained, nor can it be contained in words.

Ansel Adams

All verbal analysis tends to make implicit, part conscious experiences explicit and fully conscious and to destroy them in the process. There seems to be a kind of biological rivalry between the eye and the vocal chords, epitomised by the painter puffing at his pipe in contemptuous silence while the garrulous art critic is holding forth.

Arthur Koestler

Koestler's image of the pipe puffing artist is quaintly out of date but the sentiment continues to hold true.

In spite of the above quotations a kind of tyranny of theory is on the rise. In some parts of the design education world written theory is beginning to dominate academic practice and words are becoming more important than design. There is an increasing sense that ideas are 'importantly' expressed only in written form and that a token gesture for the actual design is acceptable; a diagram will suffice. This in turn implies that ideas on their own and unmediated are sufficient and that it is somehow no longer necessary to translate and test those ideas, to any serious degree, through the medium of an actual three-dimensional form. This suggests that the idea is separate from the object and the object is a secondary carrier, that the medium is not integral to the idea. In some areas it is even being contemplated, quite seriously, that perhaps it does not matter if the design is poor so long as the student can express their ideas well in writing. This is simply unacceptable and disingenuous; implying that written material can be delivered as a valid 'substitute' for competent and articulate practice. In this world words are only intentions, and as Picasso notes, "intentions are not sufficient".

Pressure to write more and design less means that the narrative around an object becomes more important than the narrative embedded within the object. In this context even when a story is produced visually the object is inserted into the story rather than story inserted into the object.

Would it be said, for example, of a graduating music student that to play badly is acceptable as long as he/she can 'read' music? Would it be said of a surgeon that, provided his/her theoretical understanding was sound, poor scalpel work could be excused? The answer is surely clear in both cases. This is not to deny the value of theory but to assert that it must be balanced and deployed in the service of articulate practice. It is starting to be given inappropriate emphasis, and is rapidly becoming an end in itself. In art and design education it is time to put the associated theory that is taking a disproportionate hold back into reasonable perspective. Over-reliance on theory at the expense of critical practice is an evasion. Clearly one should be knowledgeable about one's subject, its history, currency, and the associated contexts in which it operates, but this knowledge and the understanding of theory should find its expression when articulated through actual design work. Writing with its own sets

of rules and protocols is a different discipline and should not become a diversionary or surrogate activity.

Real demonstration of art and design creativity is in the delivery of intelligent visual discourse through the medium of three-dimensional form. Intelligent visual discourse is the demonstration of comprehension. It is within this form of discourse that the greater proportion of time should be spent in developing and fine-tuning grammar, structure and content.

Part of the drive to elevate theory seems to stem from a desire to give creative practice 'intellectual' credibility. Creative practice, however, should not need to borrow this intellectualism from literacy. To borrow is to compromise and lose authenticity and integrity. Creative practice must claim intelligibility on its own ground and on its own terms.

In addition, making as a generative form of expressive, conceptual intent has been confused historically with making as an operation of repetitive, manual labour. 'Repetitive' is the key word here. Repetitive labour, questionably but invariably, implies doing without thinking. 'Manual' also suggests

something less cerebral, that when the hands are in operation the head is disengaged. Making something for the first time as an original, however, is no different in manual terms to writing; a physical act of conception whether with hammer, glue gun, pen or word processor: thinking directly through doing.

Importantly a distinction is being made here between critical, creative practice and commercial or vocational practice. Practice in design is often assumed to be wholly given over to basic pragmatism and expedient commerce and therefore, by association, is judged intellectually less pure than theory. Not all practice is 'corrupted' by these concerns. Academic practice should primarily be concerned with testing, revalidating or updating the fundamentals; with the development of formal languages and cultural associations and connections. Academic practice has a duty to be culturally pertinent, to connect and to challenge.

Real education in any field starts with fundamentals, learning to walk before running. Infants observe and mimic, they consolidate by repetition and practice, and they can understand the names of many things before they choose to speak. They can demonstrate this understanding by action before word. Real

education starts with making connections between
the real world of objects and the interior world
of thought.

So, it is important to begin with some basic truths.
Ideas expressed in words are not design. An idea
that might become an object is precisely that, an
idea. It is a latent possibility only, no more and no
less. It may hold tantalising promise; it may be
loaded with all kinds of associations and possibilities,
but that is all they are: untested possibilities. This is
the seductive trap. In the mind an idea can live safe
and unmolested. It has no physical dimensions, no
physical attributes.

An object is different; it has three dimensions. You
can walk around an object and establish a fairly
immediate sense of its wholeness. You can pick it up,
feel its weight, the texture and temperature of its
surface; you can discover parts, contours and edges.
You can pick up the fragrance of its materials. You
can explore its exterior. Often, but not always, you
can open it up or break it apart and look at its
insides. Sometimes you can uncover its structure
and find out how it works or how the parts connect
together. All of this is tangible, visceral, tactile
experience. We confront the sharp, brittle, soft, shiny,

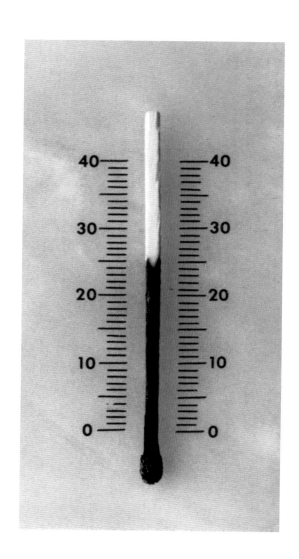

bright coloured, pungent, heavy thing-ness of the object. Similarly you can walk through a space, look up, over, forward and backwards. You can hear the echo of your own presence and footfall; feel the promise of an open light filled space around the next corner. You can breathe the texture of the weather and smell the collective ambience of place.

These are real physical experiences involving the three dimensions of space, a fourth dimension of time and five senses. Operating with this multi-sensory palette is what idea, articulated as form, represents. If an object attempts to embody certain ideas and associations we are in a position to evaluate whether the object achieves those ambitions well or poorly. Does it speak visually, resonate, trigger memory or is its appearance vacant, dissonant or incomprehensible? Is there a visual story, coherence, poetic tension, drama, magic or are there only rudimentary connections, superficial cliches, and arbitrary confusion? If the 'grammar' of the visual is employed with intelligent purpose then it is there to be 'read' as meaningfully as any written text.

In the visual world words are best used like poisons in early medicine, sparingly with caution and restraint. They should be employed as links, titles, puns, adjuncts and bridges; aids, not substitutes.

Noguchi sculpture garden,
Long Island City, New York.

methods

Creativity is allowing yourself to make mistakes.
Art is knowing which ones to keep.
Scott Adams

There is another aspect to books about design and process that should also be discussed here. Every one wants a guidebook because guidebooks offer reassurance: where to go, what to see, how to do it, when and why. In most of these there is either an explicit or implicit promise, which, in the case of genuine creative activity, can never be delivered; follow the method and you can be assured of the 'correct' results. Unfortunately this kind of instruction works to a reasonable degree for car maintenance, modestly well for cookbooks and hardly at all for anything that might loosely be determined as inventive, creative and original.

Books about design method almost always result in a set of diagrams, which have the look of scientific formula and objective method. There is always somewhere, lodged in the text, at least one diagram with assorted words, floating and highlighted in bold, and one or more arrows. These affect to have quasi-scientific gravitas and so, by association, they must have legitimacy. The implication is: follow this system, it will keep you on the right track and deliver an appropriate solution. Checklists ask questions like "How are you going to verify your findings?" This kind of question works for science but it doesn't work for art in the same way. Design falls somewhere

between these two and hence, confusingly, sometimes a question of this kind is relevant and sometimes it is not. Ideas that work as objects and products do not always correspond to the rational logic that this kind of methodology implies. The right questions and reflective analysis sometimes have to be evolved through an exploratory process of doing, rather than reading and responding to prescribed lists.

Nevertheless books of this type insist on procedural methods and what appear so reasonably to come down to that flight of fantasy crushing term, "objective methodology". This is always deployed in the attempt to 'civilise' the process of design; to make it accessible and therefore acceptable in general society.

Methods of this kind are often used and applied in relation to commercial imperatives. They attempt to mediate between the languages of design and that of commerce, to speak some kind of design/business Esperanto. The problem with this is that this Esperanto always contains more words with business roots, than words originating from design. It is a language filled with specific, checklist forms of analysis within specific sets of predefined rules. This is always so

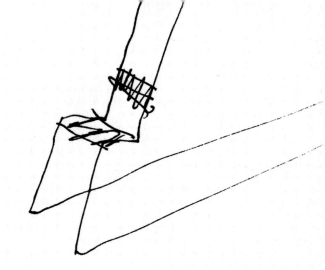

reassuringly plausible, so externally accessible, that it becomes, by default, the only way to do it. Objectivity, because of its communicable property, evolves as the only valid, guiding design principle. The effect of championing these methods, because they are understandable outwardly, is that they become internalised within design practice; they begin to dominate design method and culture. They work because they mostly produce results that are predictable, those channelled within a predetermined procedure. Follow a prescribed method and you will get a proscribed result. What you will very rarely get is some genuinely new insight or a fresh way of looking at the world.

There are many successful businesses run by entrepreneurs, who often ignore established business protocol and operate on hunches and intuitions. Despite this, intuition and the non-rational are not trusted in the mainstream, accounting world of business. Less formal, less well understood, less apparently reliable, they rarely appear in any design method book because they cannot be quantified. They do not conform to the rules, the pervasive ubiquitous and subliminal rules of objectivity, and so they are consciously or unconsciously suppressed.

One of the great, inadvertent casualties of design method is the denial of subjectivity as an active tool.

It is denied mostly because method is often confused with result. If the method is not rational how is it possible that the result can be? If we do not fully understand the method how can we be sure of the result? The answer is that results can be assessed on their own merits and failings. Results achieved by whatever means still have to stand up to scrutiny by whatever criteria are relevant.

The fact is that Western culture has found itself in an environment completely overrun by uncultivated languages and modes of conduct produced by industry itself. These changes are much more far-reaching, vital, and effective than the ones Western culture had itself devised. So it was that out of this unease, out of the capacity of culture to keep abreast of the changing times, the avant-garde was born as a traumatic recovery, as a creative spark flashing between two masses moving at different velocities. The avant-garde served as a sort of recovery room for the modern culture, a place of high creative tension that permitted the modes and languages of art – out of step with a rapidly changing world – to catch up.

It is true that the way in which the avant-garde affected this linkup between culture and reality has always been marked by a bewildering increase in irrationality. These elements of the irrational are actually the fruit of the effort to discover more wide-ranging methodologies that contain a higher degree of reality, thereby expanding the instruments of work so that they are also capable of embracing the 'irrational' which makes up such a large part of reality. In actual fact the terms' irrational', illogical', and 'heretical' are merely definitions of processes or languages that are not provided for, which already exist outside officially accepted patterns and schemes.

Andrea Branzi

If this still has a residual trace of 'head in the clouds' it is important to add clear qualification. The use of 'irrational' methods such as subjectivity and intuition do not mean that anything goes. The embracing of

subjectivity does not mean handing oneself over to self-indulgent caprice and whim: nor does it mean the indiscriminate feeding of personal idiosyncrasy. It means that intuition can and should be acknowledged and used for what it is or at least what it appears to be; a sense of the rightness of something ahead of the proof or verification. It means trusting that we will find that elusive rationalisation, currently invisible to the conscious mind, of something clearly and positively convincing to us in every sense, except that which can be explained. This is akin in feeling to seeing a person clearly in the minds eye but whose lost name is teetering on the tip of the tongue. It means that we might only know the meaning of what we have done after we have done it; by a kind of retrospective analysis of where we have been and what it communicates back to us. Theory in this sense comes after practice and informs subsequent practice. This form of contemplation and analysis is a kind of slow motion replaying of the 'speed of light' synaptic click across the brain, so fast and convincing that we believe before we know why.

Recognition of this suggests that we do not need to have a complete list of dos and don'ts before we set out. Anyone can throw away someone else's rulebook provided that they take personal responsibility for writing an equally rigorous rulebook of their own on the journey. You can have your head in the clouds provided that your feet are on the ground, on the common ground walked by everyman.

It has often been said not always with admiration that Charles Eames designed for himself. So he did, but in this above all he was conscious of discipline, restraint and responsibility.

> We like to think that we design for ourselves, and we do. But in the important ways we are really very much like a lot of other people. And if you are going to design for yourself then you have to make sure that you design deeply for yourself because otherwise you are just designing for your eccentricities and that is where you are different.

Charles Eames

Christopher Frayling, Rector of the Royal College of Art, is fond of quoting a line which he claims is from EM Forster's aunt: "How can I tell what I think until I see what I say?" Translated into creative design terms this apparently paradoxical statement is another way of expressing trust in an unconscious organising process. Trust in going ahead and doing something guided by intuition in order then to find out, post-rationally, what the unconscious has revealed.

commerce and concept

Computers are useless. They can only give you answers.

Pablo Picasso

Commerce at the expense of everything else restricts and compromises the broader idealistic interests of art and design. To a large degree design has lost its pioneering, questioning edge. Increasingly, design colleges in tandem with design practices talk about strategy, strategic positioning and brand values more often than cultural values. "What is your target audience?" is a contextual question asked more frequently than "What is your ideological position?" Market economy is driving all before it and commercial worth is increasingly taking precedence over cultural value.

Both the grand and intimate design narratives of Modernism and Postmodernism have made way for manipulative, commercial realism. What started out with noble, social and cultural intentions has now often been compromised and corrupted for expedient financial gain. Mass production, laudably, equals accessible prices for all and leads to mass consumption. Mass production, however, becomes a victim of its own success, we have more than we need and most of it works at an optimum level. Mass production now needs to create false desires, unneeded products with which to feed ego not ethos. Credit becomes a drug offered in ever increasing doses to produce and feed an addictive need for more consumption. More consumption, in turn, produces a mass devaluing of the ever increasing, products manufactured.

Idealism, which survives its formative struggle, almost always descends into rule bound ideology, and the restrictive dogma of modernism's abstract, visual palette has been questioned and challenged. However, both its original, genuinely idealistic optimism and the pluralistic, multi-layered remedies of Postmodernism have been replaced, mostly with a knowing cynicism. In a contemporary Western culture with fewer genuine needs to satisfy, more often than not when design climbs into bed with mainstream commerce, manipulative exploitation is born. Branding, an embryo when mass production first realised it had to differentiate the general uniformity of its output, is now a colossus dominating cultures of consumption. Many products are externally or artificially positioned or superficially contextualised. The skins of most products are designed to accommodate and resonate with entirely fabricated and bogus narratives. Often not even the skin is changed. The product is merely 'repositioned', inserted into a feel-good story and carried along for the ride: heroics produced by association and osmosis.

Genuine impulses of wonder, mystery, magic and sensuality have been trapped and encoded, turned into sound bites and 30 second special effects. Effects spin into tenuous clouds like so much candyfloss, big on spectacle, small on nutritious substance. Superficiality is flaunted and celebrated. Terms like 'eye candy' are used without apparent irony, magazines call themselves names such as *wallpaper** and tout aspirational, inaccessible fantasies. Furniture, space, and 'lifestyle' are consumed as images over and over and over again. Surface covers surface and however hard we dig, we are always in the same insecure and insubstantial place. Baudrillard's "precession of simulacra" is upon us. Manufacturing and selling has been replaced by marketing, quantity has become a quality, surface replaces substance.

In contrast, Eames' short animated film *Powers of Ten* tells us a great deal about scale and mathematics with sublime, visual elegance and spellbinding simplicity.

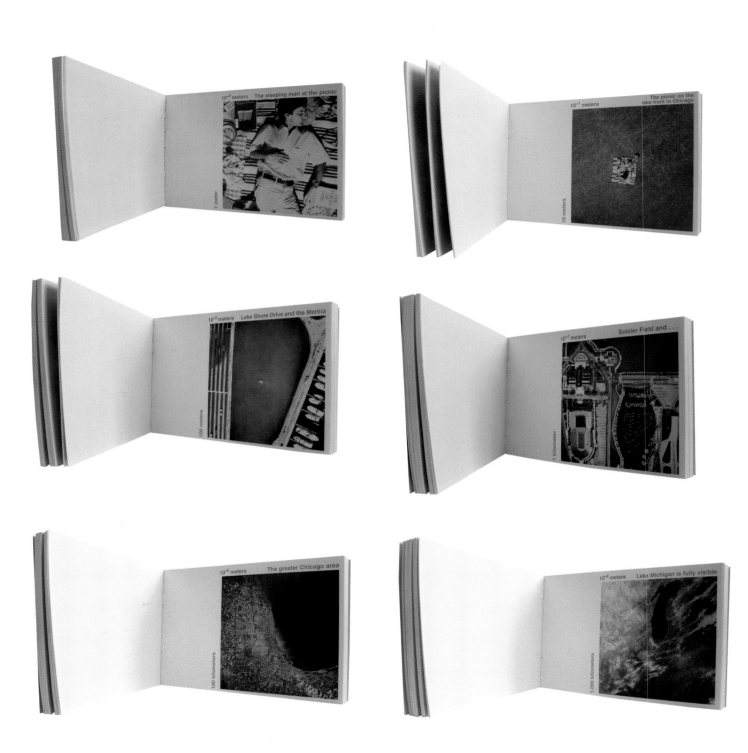

10^{0} meters   The sleeping man at the picnic

1 meter

10^{+1} meters   The picnic on the lake front in Chicago

10 meters

10^{+2} meters   Lake Shore Drive and the Marina

100 meters

10^{+3} meters   Soldier Field and . . .

1 kilometer

10^{+5} meters   The greater Chicago area

100 kilometers

10^{+6} meters   Lake Michigan is fully visible

1,000 kilometers

Powers of Ten: a Film Dealing with the Relative Size of Things in the Universe and the Effect of Adding Another Zero

At the beginning of the animation the camera frames one square metre of ground from one metre above the ground. The camera tracks vertically upward and away from the ground travelling to a height of ten metres in ten seconds. It continues tracking away vertically travelling to a height of 100 metres in the next ten seconds. In the subsequent ten second period it reaches 1,000 metres and so on increasing in one power of ten for every ten second time period. The effect is a perception of increasing speed effected by smooth gear changes at the boundaries of each power of ten distance. In the film, each of these boundary points is indicated by a square which gradually recedes in diminishing perspective.

The sequence extrapolates out to 10^{25} metres or one billion light years before falling back through the galaxies and returning to earth. At one metre above the ground it begins the journey (again in ten second increments) down to ten centimetres, one centimetre, one millimetre and on in and ever slower decent into the microscopic world of cells, molecules, atoms, protons and neutrons. From 10^{25} to 10^{-16} this is a spellbinding and almost infinite journey in comparative magnitudes; scientific information delivered with poetic vision.

10^{+7} meters — The Earth

10,000 kilometers

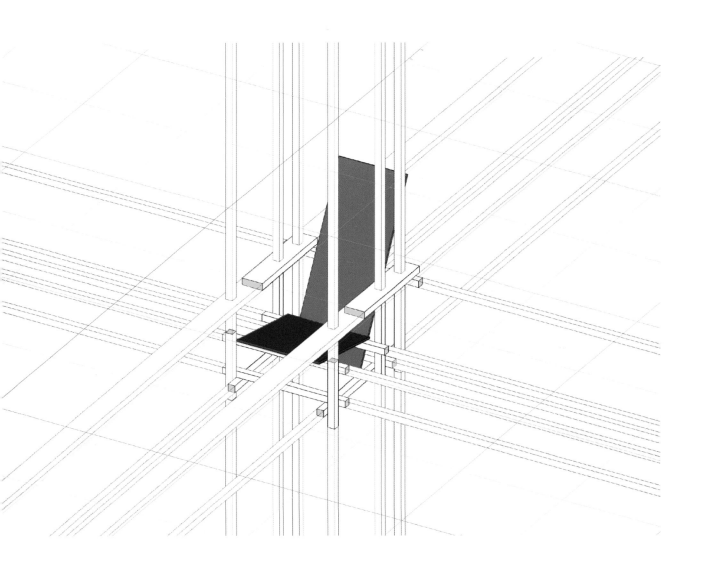

Mixing Rietveld's abstraction with
more concrete domestic cultural
associations relating to chairs might
produce ideas like this. Other layers
of information and meaning are
added and the conceptual austerity
of Rietveld's original teeters on the
edge of the cosy domesticity of the
three-piece suite.

Contrast also some of the most potent and enduring
icons of design. Many of these had nothing to do
with the 'fabricated desires' of the marketplace; they
were idea driven. They were pure experiment for its
own sake; to see what could be done, how far a
structure could be reduced to rudimentary building
blocks; to pursue economy of form, often but not
always aligned to economy of production, or to push
a material to its limits.

Gerrit Rietveld's iconic Red Blue Chair, for example,
grew out of formal rationalisation, the abstract
construction of chair form. In this design the
seat and back are reduced to a physical and
diagrammatic expression of the Cartesian co-
ordinates, height, width and depth. This is chair
as pure abstraction.

axioms and values

Those who do not want to imitate anything, produce nothing.

Salvador Dali

Spaceships and time machines are no escape from the human condition. Let Othello subject Desdemona to a lie-detector test; his jealousy will still blind him to the evidence. Let Oedipus triumph over gravity; he won't triumph over his fate.

Arthur Koestler

It is often assumed that creativity is best delivered from a clean sheet, starting from first principles, or that 'newness' means employing the latest technology. It is probable that these assumptions stem from powerful Modernist axioms like Gropius' "starting from zero" and "continuous revolution". These and the many others of Modernism deployed at the time were rhetorically useful in breaking the decadence of a level of ornamental embellishment, which had lost touch with any kind of meaningful narrative. For example, "Ornament and Crime" (an Adolph Loos essay title often misquoted as "Decoration is a Crime") lines up in seamless correspondence with Constantin Brancusi's "Truth to Materials" to support the concept of the pure and the uncontaminated.

Axioms are like super-condensed methodology books. In relation to original creativity treat with caution! The values and limitations of the aesthetics of Modernism have been well documented elsewhere. In architecture its attempt to avoid style simply produced a style *sans* decoration, using the 'pragmatism' of the factory building as a model; a variation on earlier classical styles. In design the products followed the contents of the factory, the machinery. A 'machine aesthetic' derived forms from the fundamental, mechanical geometries of the devices that made them. Constructed of cogs, wheels, pulleys and pistons, machines typically converted linear or oscillating motion to circular motion and conversely circular motion to linear. In turn designers converted these up and down, side to side, round and round characteristics into products whose formal combinations of shape were based on cone, cylinder, sphere, pyramid and cube, the latter being the most basic of platonic solids. The combined effect of these axioms still reverberates and the impression that originality should, in some fundamental sense, be uncontaminated by the decorated styles of the past still persists.

Venturi and Rauch, Franklin Court

Franklin Court in Philadelphia is the original site of Benjamin Franklin's home and print house. When it was proposed to build a Franklin museum on the site one possibility under serious consideration was to build a replica of the original Franklin dwellings. The architect Robert Venturi argued that a replica can only be a facsimile, a fake, and can never truly replicate with legitimate authenticity the real thing. The fake tricks and cheats the imagination because the real materials, methods, smells, sounds and other ambient details have been long lost, dissolved and dissipated in the ruins of the site. The best way to invoke the past is to activate, engage and excite the imagination. And one of the best ways to do that is to allude poetically to things no longer present. Venturi proposed a drawing as an object. The Franklin dwellings as three-dimensional frames drawn in space to the real external dimensions of the original buildings thus producing a ghost or put more benignly a spirit occupying the same volume and position as the original dwellings.

Within this frame, in various positions in the interior space, are stones let into the ground and inscribed with correspondence. The writings are Benjamin Franklin's and all are selected because they refer directly to objects and attributes, which were in and of this house. He writes about his desk and how pleased he is with it; about a particular view or an aspect of the garden. These writings are located in the footprints that the objects referred to might have occupied. A past building whose foundations have been covered by time's erosion has to be re-excavated. Venturi locates the real museum under the ground of the site, in an archaeological metaphor which allows plenty of space to tell Franklin's history and legacy while preserving the scale of the original site above.

In 1966 the architect Robert Venturi, in the opening sentences of his seminal book *Complexity and Contradiction in Modern Architecture*, famously paraphrased Mies van der Rohe's by then almost sacred mantra of Modernism "less is more" with the scandalously blasphemous "less is a bore". Venturi's book questioned the restrictive palette of Modernism and framed a manifesto for what came to be known as Postmodern architecture and design. This book and a subsequent one, *Learning from Las Vegas*, responded to the change in value as high and low art, the gallery and the commercial street, came together in the 'Pop' art and design of the period. However, Venturi's intentions were often misinterpreted and corrupted into a kind of mix and match palette of architectural style. Venturi's historical and commercial architectural analysis wished to replace abstract form with symbolic form in a contemporary context.

In our experiments with Form follows Idea it is interesting to similarly replace Loos' "Ornament and Crime" with "Ornament and Rhyme", Gropius' "Starting from Zero" with "Starting from One Hundred Thousand", to find out where they lead using a variety of associations and references which operate beyond both the formal abstraction of Modernism and the style manipulation of the Postmodern.

> What for many others was the idea of progression was for him the transgression namely, the question of what, as yet unnoticed possibilities lie within this thing or that. How can it be seen? How can it be represented? What follows from this representation? This is an attitude that places reaction ahead of action and Munari welcomes the impulse of anything that results in a surprised reaction, which can also include the past tradition, the existing culture of everyday life. The original element must always remain visible or tangible behind the outer layer of the image. He is interested in transparency, in the transformation that is also recognizable as such and the simultaneous juxtaposition of the original material and the new object that has been derived from it.

Bruno Munari

Exploring the poetics of the everyday and valuing what we have already does not mean a reactionary

stance against progress. It means being reflective about the headlong pursuit of progress and innovation at all costs. We should be cultivating simple and profound awareness and recognising that many innovations, especially in the arts, are not innovations in the pure sense of the word but reinterpretations of the same issues for new generations. Reinterpretation means recognition that the fundamentals do not change. We still have to eat, sleep, protect ourselves from the elements, and wonder about the stars in the night sky. It means also being mindful that we do not throw the baby out with the bathwater. Tragically memory and reflection are in short supply and if history teaches us anything it teaches us that mostly we fail to value what we have until it is too late.

Progress and tradition are in eternal conflict yet both should be framed in a generously large context allowing for distance and perspective. Wisdom resides in recognising, respecting and reconciling the sometimes polarised virtues of each. This occasionally means practising creative optimisation rather than formal compromise. Often a kind of poetic, conceptual optimisation resides in objects and propositions, which are paradoxical.

Paradoxically, paradox and ambiguity used in the right context can work to reveal and illuminate, and to reconcile opposites in a holistic way. They give shape to overlapping and contradictory issues which pragmatic and pedestrian delivery often fails to achieve. For an idea to really speak as an object, that is, a thing in three dimensions, it must have more than one dimension. This may seem like an obvious thing to say. Reference here, however, is to dimensions of meaning and association, correspondences of

material and context, in addition to the more obvious and inescapable physical dimensions. An idea with several 'value' dimensions or layers is more likely, on balance, to be rich and intriguing. This does not mean that complex ideas are better or more interesting than simple ones. Nor does it mean that complex forms stand for complex ideas. Simple forms may contain complex or profound ideas, and conversely, complex forms may be merely an attempt to dress up and elaborate a fundamentally one-dimensional idea. For an idea to have several dimensions means that there has to be space within its realisation for interpretation or contemplation.

There is, of course, a balance to be struck. Building layers and dimensions is no place for the random or the intellectually sloppy. Complexity and contradiction have to be handled with skill. Overload an object with too many layers and associations and it will collapse under a weight of arbitrary confusion. Selective contradiction, however, can add rich conceptual texture, elusive magic, and sensations hard to define in words.

> I like complexity and contradiction in architecture. I do not like the incoherence or arbitrariness of incompetent architecture nor the precious intricacies of picturesqueness or expressionism. Instead I speak of a complex and contradictory architecture based on the richness and ambiguity of modern experience, including that experience which is inherent in art.
>
> Robert Venturi

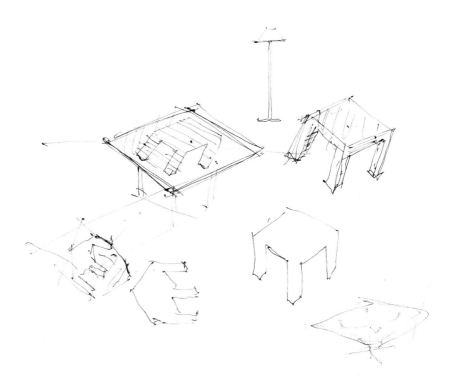

Clearly there are appropriate and inappropriate vehicles for this. Some places are no places for ambiguity. The pilot's instrument panel on a jumbo jet, for example, needs to be glare free. It is required to be an excellent example of face value clarity; the epitome of legibility. The last thing needed here is ambiguity! No layers of meaning, no poetic conundrums are valid. There should be no room for any interpretation other than the right one.

On the other hand where stakes are less safety-critical, good visual ideas can be multi-layered and poetic. As such they slip across boundaries and cover different territories simultaneously. They are able to construct 'never before seen' interpretations of things we have seen before; things that we know but haven't thought of yet. They are often impervious to literary categorisation. As can often

be demonstrated with literary texts rewritten in different languages, the meaning can be lost in translation. *Déjà vu* and *zeitgeist* are words which inhabit the English language but remain in their native tongue because there are no single words in English which succinctly express these concepts.

Also, there are often no rules other than those which are determined by the frame of the idea. In this context it follows also that there is no allegiance to any material, method, formal language or ideology. If the central idea is the telling of a visual story then it may employ any cultural, typological, symbolic or metaphoric element to articulate its message. "Truth to materials" can be recast as "truth to idea".

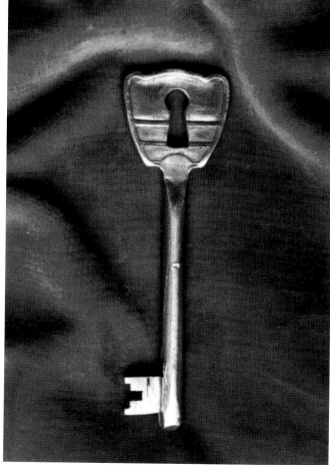

familiar and unfamiliar artificial and natural

I love the idea of slowness. It took thousands of years to come to the conclusion that we think of as a chair. Vitra moves fast in comparison to that, but I do think that every object has a natural evolutionary pace. If Charles Eames had said, "We have to finish it fast fast fast!" his chairs wouldn't be relevant a half-century later. I believe in getting things right. In our industry, you can't force something if you want it to be good. It has to become. Every object is a being with a soul. Our work is to find that soul. Sometimes we can't manage to find it, and we have to abandon the project or try again. We're not worried about being first to market, because what we do is unique by its very nature. Good design is relevant for decades; a year matters little on that scale.

Rolf Fehlbaum

Forms never materialise out of thin air, totally unrecognisable, like aliens from another planet. Even aliens in movie fiction, however extreme, have recognisable features, extrapolated from the familiar elements of our world. We attempt to understand the new by relating it to forms and ideas that are familiar. Similes and metaphors, both literal and visual, act like bridges to link the unknown back to the known.

Furniture typologies – chair, table, shelf, etc. – and their respective sub-categories – dining chair, office chair, coffee table, conference table, etc. – are what we have chosen to call "mature object types". Mature, because their general form and genre are well established and culturally embedded: we recognise them. The underlying formal relationships of function and form have been used and verified over many generations; they have been around for thousands of years. The same is true of vessels, cups and bowls for drinking and holding liquids. These represent another example of a mature type because there is a consistent base form underlying all the nuances of diverse cultural embellishment.

Contrast this with what could correspondingly be defined as immature typologies. Immature types never get the chance to mature because changes in technology or behaviour cause these forms to morph into other significantly different shapes. The underlying 'services' provided by these ephemeral devices remain constant but the delivery platform shape-shifts. For example, mechanical writing was first produced by type-setting on a printing press, and subsequently with the typewriter, which was superseded by the word processor, whose keyboard will surely be replaced by sophisticated voice recognition software. Recorded and reproduced sound started with the hand cranked wax cylinder,

Message exchange
Installation within the Benjamin Franklin Museum beneath the site of Franklin's House and Print Works. One manifestation of the changing shape of telephone communication.

changed into the vinyl record and magnetic tape, and was followed later by video tape, the compact disc, the digital video disc and the memory chip. Each of these memory devices has its own corresponding decoder or player and respectively each of these had its own form. In every case, ease, speed and convenience drive the integration of the new offspring; earlier forms become redundant or are withdrawn from production to make way for the newer, more 'advanced' techno forms. These types of object keep changing their form because of convenience, but the underlying service remains constant. In the above examples, mechanical writing and recorded replicable sound are ends which remain the same. Form and behaviour in relation to it changes with some frequency whilst the underlying service function does not. These products have yet to evolve into mature types with fixed and unambiguous identities. By the time we have learned

to recognise them they have slipped away to be replaced by a new, equally ephemeral type. These immature types include a variety of electronic devices, which on the whole have indeterminate identities. The keypad is a common element in products with a wide range of contrasting function. Who can tell, for example, the generic difference between a mobile phone, a calculator and a TV remote control? The increasing miniaturisation of the inside working parts, and electronics having replaced mechanics, mean that these devices can be any shape and size, so what shape and size should they be given that they represent different activities and functions? The ambiguity of the shapes above suggests that this question is still open.

In the history of the human race, communicating 'complex' messages quickly over distances greater than shouting range is a relatively recent

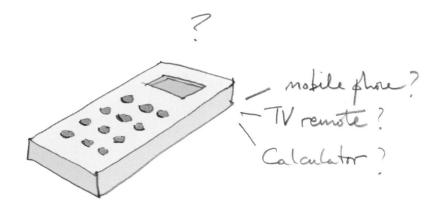

development (assuming we count drums and smoke signals as relatively limited in range and subtlety, and semaphore as relatively slow). The defining issue is communication, and no underlying form has emerged from within the diverse range of delivery systems on offer. In formal terms the ancestors of the mobile phone, as a long distance communication device, are landline, megaphone Morse code, messages tied to homing pigeons, arrows, runners, smoke signals and drums: shapes and methods of great diversity.

The mobile phone itself has a form which is still changing shape; with progressive chip technology, it will become ever more miniature and voice activated. It can become increasingly invisible because it is the disembodied service of communication, the transmission of talking and listening, which is the essential defining element, not the shape of the communication device. The eventual emergence of some form of implant, activated mentally, seems

almost inevitable. This, after a range of electronic piercing versions have staked out base camp on the skin and consolidated the bridge between inner and outer body. We are already on the way; piercing and tattoos are increasingly a much greater part of mainstream Western culture across both gender and class.

The predominant symbol for 'telephone' shows an arched element with blobs at both ends hovering horizontally above a round disc with radially pierced holes. The arched element represents a handset with end blobs of ear and mouthpiece, while the disc symbolises the dial element. Yet the three-dimensional form of telephone that this symbol represents no longer exists. Currently neither of these shapes is found in the mainstream product output of either mobile or landline telephones. It persists as a symbol presumably because the shape is sufficiently distinctive to be differentiated from other hand held keyboard operated types as 'telephone'.

No mass produced telephone looks like this any more.

Generic 'keypad'.

Chema Madoz
An alternative and poetic delivery of a remote control. The shape is changed from the generic to something that more graphically captures the associations of its use in relation to the TV screen... zapping the channels.

The convenience and ease of use of a mature typology in contrast does not change and does not have to rely on secondary symbols, or informative names printed on the product. The approximately horizontal platform to sit on and the approximately vertical back to lean against, have been resting legs and conferring status for thousands of years. The underlying form is recognisable and does not change because of changes in technology. It does not need to be decoded. The basic relationship to the body of this support platform has been essentially constant since the ancient Egyptians.

Mature typologies are latent with expressive possibilities for poetry, humour and criticism far richer than have so far been explored. These types because of their generic familiarity allow formal investigation and questioning of cultural values, consumption, mass marketing, aspirational branding, and so on to be explored directly through the visual information within and associated with the objects themselves.

Concrete counterweight on tipping bridge, Mystic, Connecticut.

paper
light shade
corrugated card.
neoprene

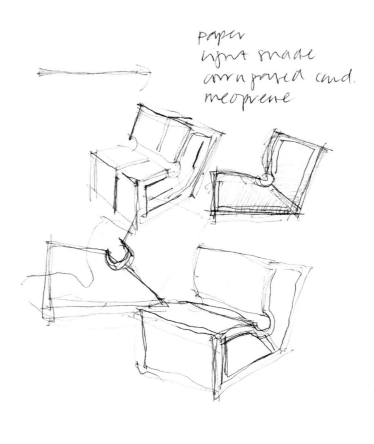

Max Chairs, 2002

In an era of lightweight minimality these chairs deliberately set out to articulate the idea of mass. The space between the seat platform and the ground is filled. The same equivalent space is filled behind the backrest and the two delineated areas are joined together on an axis dividing the angle between seat and back. The resultant form is reinterpreted with the intention of maintaining 'mass' as an embodied idea. Ideas including physical weight, sandwiched density, extra thickness, mass media and quantity of material are used to represent and deliver mass.

Different materials configure the form in different ways: steel acrylic and feathers, slabs of Norwegian fir, solid cork, sandwiched cardboard, paper and upholstered foam.

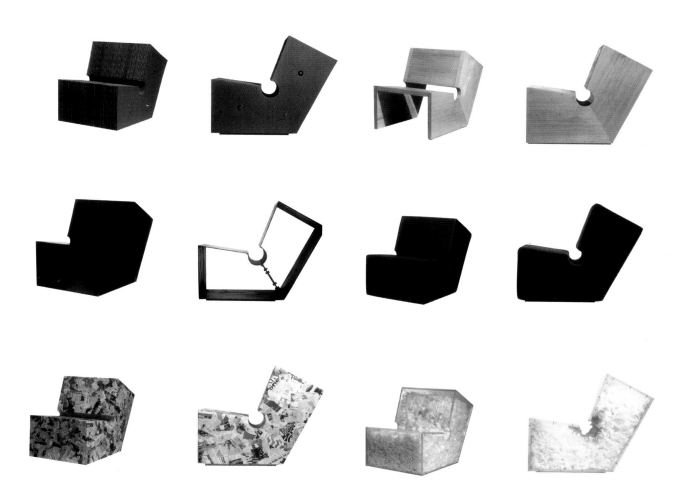

These lamps contrast opposite visual associations: the idea of light, lightness and airiness with the idea of mass, weight and the solidity of the ground. Light here is carried on massive trunk-like columns of rusted steel. At the base, heavy, flat plates of steel make emphatic and broad contact with the ground. The lights themselves are pregnant forms laying horizontally on their cylindrical plinths.

This is a kind of methodology which asks the artefact to be introspective, to contemplate itself. It is one where the purpose is to work directly with objects as 'information'. Meaningful shapes over 'nice' shapes, legitimate, authentic associations rather than superficial, contrived, marketing led ones; what they represent, and their nature and cultural context. Articulating types so that they will speak not just eloquently, in the sense of proportion, balance and structural integrity, but also informatively about themselves, their use and their cultural associations, in their own visual language. Mature artifacts are in the secure position of being simultaneously able to function and act as commentary on their function. They have recognisable status and in that sense have the authority to be critical of their own generative culture.

Within this activity the product can be moved from its role as 'passive servant' to 'active commentator'. Design becomes poetic and rhetorical and this in turn generates a richer language of design.

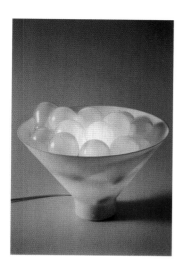

Golden Delicious, 1997-98
From a collection called Light and Shade: in this collection the relationship between light and shade is reconfigured to tell different stories about the culture of light. Golden Delicious explores introspectively the Modernist axioms "truth to materials" and "less is more". The shade (a light container) is inverted to become a bowl, literally and physically a container of light. Many bulbs piled over one central lit bulb become a collective diffuser; light source (bulb) becomes light shade; the humble bulb a desirable fruit. Paradoxically this piece has both an absurd and a legitimate integrity... delicious. Manufactured by Ligne Roset.

Transparent Table, 1997
Taking "form follows function" and "less is more" to absurdly logical extremes, the meaning and function of this table is as explicitly 'clear' as it can be. The legs–glass cleaning bottles–support and maintain the glass top. Glass tops are often a pretext for the display of legs. Here the legs ensure their own visibility. Mr Muscle is the 'clear' choice for the cleaning bottle brand because of the name's implied supporting leg strength. The table is self-supporting, self-cleaning, self-sustaining, self-promoting and self-evident... transparent.

Power Tower, 1998

Power Tower uses the banal and generic fittings (lighting plugs, sockets and bulbs) and reconfigures them in a more 'poetic light'. The tower makes play with the idea of adjustability within a mechanistic rather than electronic idiom—sockets are mounted in four orientations, cables to the bulbs are flexible. Thus it is a kind of retrospective track lighting system, one which could have existed before track lighting; an absurd extrapolation into the past; something accessible in an analogue and pre-electronic/digital world.

Generator, 1997

Formal correspondences between the spout of a watering can and a par 38 spotlight: water and light, the essential ingredients for life, come together.

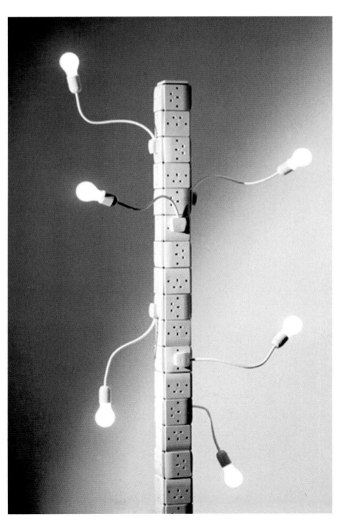

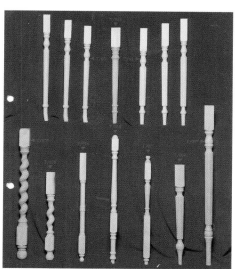

The Archaeology of Style, 1998
Glass topped tables are about showing the legs, or saying something about transparency and minimality. Here is a table for really showing off table legs—a catalogue of styles to end all style—dead legs, bleached, discarded style bones, all lying down to be superseded by the next generation. In one sense it is the definitive glass topped coffee table, since conceptually it is implied that the table is infinite, extending down into the past and up into the future and containing all the legs that ever were and ever will be designed. In the archaeology of style we are viewing just a core sample.

 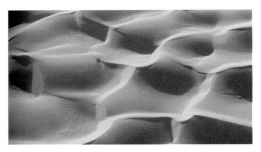

poetics of the everyday: natural forces

These images and designs illustrate another interpretation and expression of the poetics of the everyday. They make use of the everyday availability of natural forces in the delivery of formal expression. The resulting forms represent the use of minimal means on material, and making the material shape itself to produce appropriate solutions.

These are natural forces at work. Forms shaped by combinations of one element acting or reacting against another – gravity, density of material, pressure – modified by a third, sharpened by a fourth, etc..

For example, place several large stones into a trickling stream and the water will flow around them, responding to the new interruption. It will flow slowly here, quickly there, probing and searching the contingencies of the modified terrain until it consolidates a new path. At that point in time, under those specific conditions that new path will always be inevitable: the best that gravity, water speed and texture of landscape will allow.

These forces are freely available but precisely because they are so universal, so general and ubiquitous, they become 'invisible', often ignored, overlooked or in some instances actively resisted.

In many cases, forms are generated with far more complicated means of production and process than is really necessary and with less authentic results.

Obeying the laws of physics is not a restriction but free assistance. Observation and acknowledgement of these forces makes them available as tools in the control and delivery of form. The flow of the river with its new stones is inevitable but 'control' lies with the choice of the particular stones, where the stones are placed, and knowledge of the materials of the terrain. The designer can choose within a set of natural dynamics; can control the amount, size, pressure, etc., of any particular element. Acknowledging the laws of physics with selective skill allows apparently effortless and fantastic magic to be performed with simple means. The images on these pages illustrate the results of observing and applying this process.

Bamboo fencing; one material but many textures and qualities. Each evolved from the direct use of the natural potential of the material.

Sand dunes shaped by wind and gravity.

Maxine Naylor, Sketch of Alexander Calder Mobile.

Alexander Calder, Mobile (detail)
Benjamin Franklin Parkway, Philadelphia.

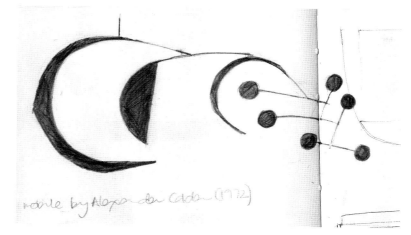

Hanging Lightscreens, 1984

The natural spring like resistance of solid section aluminium bar is used to hold the large sailcloth reflector sheets in tension. These architectural sail lamps are ornamental from beginning to end. They owe their shapes to sails, their engineering to the structure of the longbow, their aesthetic leans to Calder and their existence to the fact that lights are almost infinitely pervertable–you can do more or less what you like with them and still end up with something useful. In this example, the translucent sails of matt white sailcloth diffuse natural daylight, or part reflect and part sponge up any artificial light directed on them. The light aspect is an excuse to make poetic whimsy–almost sci-fi spaceship forms catching the solar wind.

IBM Lightwell Suspended Lightscreens, 1984

Architectural installation commission: sketches and model based on the previous hanging light screens.

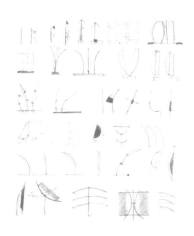

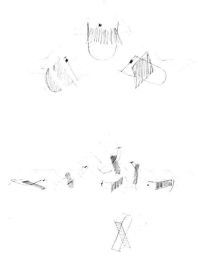

Confetti Lights, 1983
Shades are die stamped to fold into loose triangular pockets around each light. The folds employ the material's natural resilience to lock the pocket in place without any additional fastenings.

Sketch development for Sheet Lighting collection.

Bow Sheet Light, 1982
The addition of the natural bowing of resilient aluminium tubing adds an alternative means by which to shape the shade material.

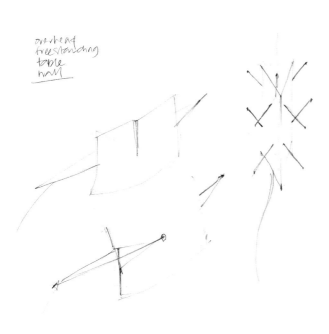

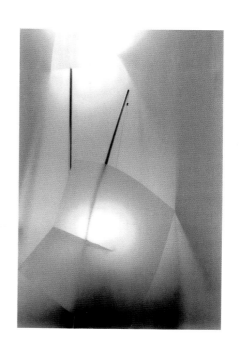

Theo Light small, 1989
The design makes elegant use of a simple, friction fixing. Fine, laser cut slots in the harder, aluminium panels position and control the natural resilience of the white, translucent diffuser material: a complex natural form from a simple method.

Theo Light large, 1989
The design is articulated using the same means of fine cut slots and friction to shape the diffuser sheets. In this example, the aluminium controlling element is set horizontally.

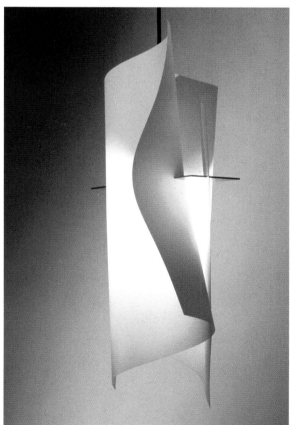

open process

Starting with intuitive guiding notes and no other instructions, we developed a process of idea generation by uncovering 'design'. This began without regard for material or market, process or position, with no detailed brief relating to the usual design parameters and checklists, with no real agenda and no predetermined manifesto other than the intuition to test our trust in intuition.

The guiding principles were:
Valuing and revaluing what we have already.
Working with found material in both component and form.

This turned out to be a process of finding ideas and of generating objects from a kind of physical expedition: a journey to the everyday world. After a while the process came to be called the "archaeology of the invisible" and its result labelled the "poetics of the everyday". The process is called this because what emerged is analogous to a kind of archaeological dig. In this case, however, the digging is in territory which is above the ground. The dig consists of looking for things that cannot be seen, paradoxically, because they are everywhere to be seen. Things, which are so common, so universally used and understood, so unassuming and so

Archeology of the Invisible
—familiarities, similarities and
differences. The bases under your
seat; elements that no one looks at.

Erich Lessing
In the garden of art dealer Friedrich Welz, 1959
These objects are a kind of rudimentary,
mechanical glue holding the world together
at a fundamental level, and the better they
work, the more invisible they are.

unobtrusive that they fade into the generalised background activity of the world.

It is in the nature of such things that they do not have 'look at me' status or presence; they will not have been designed with an eye for the design award. These are things uncontroversial; things non-provocative; things universally or culturally conformist. Things so suited to their surroundings that they sit and operate unnoticed in chameleon silence. So silent that they may as well be 'under the ground', so that the process of revealing them becomes archaeological in spirit and intent.

These things are of the same type and range as all of the 'look at me' things, which have been culturally singled out for star status. They do the same kind of jobs as the stars but they just happen to live outside of the spotlight.

It is precisely because they are not centre stage that they are taken for granted; misused, overlooked and mostly unappreciated.

Conventional archaeology performs the trick of paying attention to the ordinary like this:

Take a common object of little value, bury it in the ground for two thousand years, and dig it up again. That object, if it has slipped through time's corrosive fingers, will resonate with the patina of survival. Even if it is an ancient generation of a typology still in common use today (bowl, knife, etc.) it will have a new specificity: survivor status will be uncommon in the contemporary world. Despite having a recognisable everyday utility it will not be allowed to re-enter a functional utility place in the culture that rescues it. It will no longer be employed in such a banal and pragmatic manner. It re-enters the world anointed with poetic ambience. It will be deified, laid to rest in a new, more luxuriously appointed tomb. A palace of the immortals: the museum.

Before unearthed objects reach their new home there are other parts to the process. They are examined, speculated upon, put back together from knowledge and guesswork.

Our working method is a similar process of finding things that are hidden and of bringing them back into sight, by reinterpreting and relocating them. Common, everyday elements, features and attributes are not always immediately valued. Comparison and speculation, prior knowledge and imagination are needed to produce a plausible interpretation and renewed appreciation. Archaeologists do this by choosing a site, physically digging material out of the ground and trying to figure out what that material might be or might have been part of, responding to the ambiguous detritus by carefully cleaning and separating an apparent uniformity of mud and colour, trying to decide where the edges are. Retracing where entropy has smudged the borders and started shuffling atoms across the line, weaving its conformist propaganda; dissembling content to its earth container. Piecing it all back together like a mysterious jigsaw puzzle with randomly shaped pieces and no image on the box.

Our method is a kind of mirror image archaeology, where some of the procedures operate in reverse. As described earlier we are working with sites above the ground and our object finds are usually fully intact, complete specimens, unseen or at least unappreciated because of their commonality. Again in a kind of archaeological reverse play, we are interested in taking them apart to find out why they were invisible and putting them back together in different ways; in ways that will make them visible again, seen afresh, as if for the first time. Ways which should not be random or arbitrary

but which are speculations, as archaeologists
might make, as to the object in question's specific
nature or culture. Looking for clues in their form
and association. Connecting and hauling them
back to the world from which they have fallen
from awareness.

It is useful here to refer to some examples of
conjecture and work that illustrate this type of
bringing to mind that which has been forgotten,
ignored or never even thought of as significant.
First Marcel Duchamp:

> He (Duchamp) managed to dedicate his
> whole life to dealing with information, the
> unconscious mind and the connections
> between the observed and the unseen. As
> Duchamp stated: "If a three-dimensional
> object casts a two-dimensional shadow,
> then why isn't a three-dimensional object
> the shadow of a fourth dimension?" He
> consistently played with this incredible
> level of dialectic and observation.

James Wines

Duchamp's statement is particularly wonderful because it speculates between the known and unknown, and extrapolates an entirely reasonable proposition by linking visible and invisible elements together.

Duchamp's Rue Larrey Door is a fantastic example of an everyday object transformed and yet staying exactly the same. It is transformed by an ordinary, exquisitely subtle, almost casual shift of location within a domestic living room. Duchamp puts the door in the exact corner of the room giving out to two openings in the adjacent walls. By this simple act he gives us, in a delicious paradox, the extraordinary doorness of doors. For when his door is fully open it is closed and when it is closed it is open. This is pure idea, pure poetics, built and functioning in the physical world. Furthermore it escapes all style considerations. It does not matter what material or colour it is. It can be red and Regency, metallic and Modern. These distinctions become irrelevant. It is the fundamental hinged panel which counts, delivered to us in its always known, but always overlooked, essential nature.

Just as Duchamp's door deals with the essential idea of doorness, SITE's architectural work explores the nature of buildings in the same conceptual manner. SITE's work has often been dismissed, by other architects, as not being real architecture. This is perhaps because it refuses to sit comfortably within either of the frames of reference for Modernist or Postmodernist architecture. It employs neither Modernist, abstract Formalism nor Postmodernist architectural style referencing. SITE's work is distinguished because it deals specifically with cultural ideas about architecture, embodied in direct narrative stories, relating what buildings do and how they are symbolised.

For example, SITE's early work dealt with commercial retail spaces, an area typically avoided by serious architects. Between 1972 and 1980 SITE were commissioned to produce a series of buildings for Best Products Co. Inc.. In this strip mall retail world, architecture is reduced pragmatically to the rudimentary task of covering the greatest area for the least cost. Typically this approach generates a big, dumb box, a large shed with no distinguishing features. Differentiation between one anonymous box and the next is delivered by a big sign on or above the facade of the building. SITE's approach is not to hide or disguise this reality, but to symbolise it directly through the very idea which this position

SITE, Tilt, 1978
Towson, Maryland.

SITE, **Indeterminate Facade, 1975**
Houston, Texas.

SITE, Notch, 1977
Sacramento, California.

embodies. SITE takes the idea of a big box and plays with ways of reviling its box-like nature. Instead of conventional door entrances they play with opening the box. They produced a series of buildings for Best Products, which explored the idea of opening the box through the very direct method of using only the material from which buildings like these were made.

The names of each showroom reinforced the 'box' concept. For example, *Tilt*, 1978, is a building box whose whole front wall has been lifted up from one corner as if by a giant hand; the whole facade is leant back against the rest of the building. This creates a way in to the box interior and expresses the box-like nature of the building simultaneously. There is a kind of artful integrity at work here: what you see is what you get, and in the process the building has become its own sign. The entrance is clearly revealed through this symbolic visual gesture. The same holds true for *Notch*, 1977, where the whole bottom corner of a building slides out on tracks to provide a way in. The line of the joint is not formal, but conceived as a crack breaking open along the natural seams of the building's tessellated brickwork construction. In *Indeterminate Facade*, 1975, the ephemeral nature of this type of basic building is expressed. The building's facade is frozen

as an incomplete wall with irregular top edge, and a fall of bricks in a cascaded pile pyramiding back up against the incomplete wall. We do not know whether the building is still in construction or whether it is being demolished. It becomes, paradoxically, a monument to ephemerality.

Highrise of Homes... is a speculative proposal by SITE, which brilliantly and playfully expresses ideas about home and location. Within modern Western living there has been a tension between the competing lures of urban and country living. The compromise, suburbia, has always fallen unsatisfactorily between the two. Neither in nor out of town it doesn't quite attain the best or worst of both worlds and is always an indistinctly bland confection, lacking centre or identity. SITE propose a solution which delivers the idiosyncrasy of individual detached country dwellings with the central convenience of urban living: stripping down the skyscraper frame to what it essentially is, a set of suspended floors, and re-conceiving them as a giant shelving unit. Onto these shelves are placed individual houses. Turning the faceless and uniform skyscraper/tower block into a richly textured statement of what the building really is... a stack of homes. In a similar manner to the examples above, our 'archaeological' method is not interested in making other object typologies from the materials found. The intention is not to make other furniture shapes or even other types of chairs from this material. On the contrary, this is a form of reconstituting and reconstructing the same chairs from their own components and cultural referents. In other words, this is not taking apart chairs and using the parts to build cars, boats, sheds, shelves, or tables.

This second definition, the making of other typologies from found materials can result in a kind of ad-hoc recycling, which produces interesting objects, but these are often one-dimensional. The defining rule if work of this type is to be 'poetic' is that there must be a conceptual link between the objects and parts that form the new object and the nature of that object. Unless there is some conceptual link then the result will merely be a clever but formally superficial confection. The idea of supporting shelves on the rungs of two parallel ladders, for example, makes use only of the form and not the information that is embodied in the idea of ladders. This would be formal re-appropriation at its most banal, in that there are no other layers or connections being activated. Alternatively conceived, these shelves could have extended beyond standing reach, legitimising the use of what ladders do, or carried aspirational material on the higher rungs. These are devices which would deliver conceptual associations and added dimensions, rationalising the use of the ladder conceptually in addition to formally.

The plastic insert of a coal effect fire is turned upside down and moved from the ground into the air. Shape and idea correspondences: the sun behind clouds is represented for what it really is: a fire in the sky.

One day I'll design the perfect paper light shade, 2000

A wire frame 'wastepaper basket' containing a light bulb set in the centre. This light is surrounded by crumpled pieces of 'paper', each piece with discarded sketch ideas for paper lights. The rejected sketch sheets function as the diffuser or shade. Thus process becomes product and a kind of perpetually renewed conceptual ideal... the perfect paper light shade! Manufactured by Ligne Roset.

Conceptual use of ladders

Chema Madoz

Another image (without need of a title).

Seven Steps to Heaven, 2002

The title Seven Steps to Heaven provides just enough words to reach enlightenment.

Wallwasher, 1987

Adjustable light; lightshade conceived as bucket. Low voltage current running through the aluminium ladder allows the shade to be moved up and down, relighting on each rung.

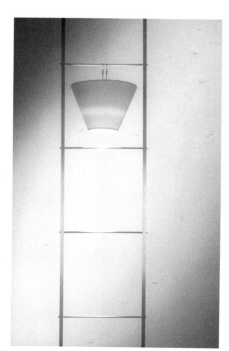

archaeology of the invisible

This final section illustrates the process of finding, deconstructing, playing with, contemplating and reconstructing some of the common chairs that populate our everyday lives. As has been noted previously these are chairs selected because their very ubiquity, their everyday ordinariness, renders them virtually invisible to notice and contemplation. This study celebrates the hidden brilliance of optimal solutions and some of the silent miracles that support our daily existence.

Each chair type is explored through a pictorial essay and the emerging chair-forms are highly theatrical manifestations of the un-theatrical; loud stories about quiet things.

All of the chairs in this collection were conceived and developed in 2003-04, and first exhibited at Salone Internationale di Mobile, Milan, in 2004.

chair types

stacking chairs

These chairs are common and are found in abundance crowding the rooms and halls of many institutions. They are cheap and serviceable.

This type of chair stacks quickly and efficiently, reducing its collective footprint to increase the available space. A stack is not just a random pile, it is an organised pile, and stacking chairs are part of specialised species of nesting pile. Nesting piles are made from objects of the same shape, which sit partly inside one another. They typically have some kind of tapering form, which allow one to easily fall into place over another. Buckets, plant pots, dishes employ this elegantly simple mechanism. The tapering element ensures that the stack is both self- locating and self-spacing.

With stacking chairs there is always some form of open taper contrived within the design. The density of the stack is determined by the degree of taper and thickness of the chair's structure. The stacking chair is a self locating component. This is absolute and simple magic, but it is not often seen or appreciated. It is the consequence of stacking we notice and not the means. We are aware of the newly available space but not the stack of chairs.

greystack

Greystack plays with the injection moulded seat/back plastic shells of these chairs in contrast to the leg structures expressed in Blackstack.

blackstack

Blackstack draws attention to the unnoticed configuration of legs and celebrates the intricate filigree of the interlocking stack. In this piece the repetitive pattern and the invisible, simple cleverness of nesting together is expressed, steel tube on steel tube.

same difference

The injection moulded seat back shell on a tubular steel leg frame is part of the generic and invisible fabric of the cafes, schools and meeting halls of the world. It's been solved, it's cheap to produce and it works serviceably well in all of these diverse locations. These three issues are the whole point and because of them this chair type is produced in the millions.

Same Difference explores the perceptions of the generic. We assume that these chairs are all the same, but they are all different. The legs walk at different speeds and carry their shells in many different ways. They also become individual like all things through use and age.

Leg studies.

polypropagation

In this 'over ground archaeology' the way in which things are found is important to their interpretation and speculation, which will ultimately determine the reconstructed form and idea.

This chair piece is constructed, in common with the other work, mostly from anonymous chairs and chair elements; in this instance, injection moulded plastic shells taken from various chairs found in different locations around London. In addition this particular reconstruction does include one recognisable chair – 'recognisable' in that it is part of the culturally visible spectrum of acknowledged chairs. Chairs that usually have a name and a designer's name firmly attached to them. It is one of those chairs that attain the status of a design classic. As has been previously established the parameters we set for our version of archaeology are to search for the culturally buried and metaphorically invisible, in contrast to the standard archaeological convention of looking for the physically buried and literally invisible. This particular find was one of those strange and ironic in-betweens. A culturally visible chair that was, for all intents and purposes, physically buried.

Buried under broken bricks and a decomposing bag of sand and stagnant water, it was lost in the margins of long discarded activity, a victim of time's degenerate persistence, at the edge of a street market. Its surface colour had been mugged into bruised black camouflage. Its contours were similarly blurred and muddled in the indeterminate landscape of brick and stinking sand. It was dead to recognisable function and easy to miss in the adjacent life and noise of the market.

The most interesting thing about this was the particular chair that it turned out to be and the condition that it was in. It was a genuine ancestor. It was, in the current expanding generations of plastic shell chairs, an ancient but an ancient of some particular significance. Here was none other that the very first form of polypropylene, stacking shell chair designed by Robin Day in 1963. This chair is significant because it holds a pivotal position representing both an end and a beginning. It sits at the end of a distinguished series of structural seat/back shell chair experiments in many different materials, starting with Hans Coray's Landi Chair in perforated aluminium. All these experiments had one clear aim, the delivery of a contoured and continuously integrated seat/back shell at an economical cost.

Day's most economical version is the chair which, given the right material and technology, was inevitable. It marked the beginning of high volume production of chairs in plastic. The material was polypropylene and the technology was injection moulding. Known simply and pragmatically as the Polyprop Chair, Day's design was the first to combine large-scale tooling with the injection moulding process. This meant very high tool costs but a correspondingly very low unit cost for the chair shell. At the time of its first production it was probably the cheapest chair on the market.

The shell was conceived so that it could be fixed to a variety of different base supports. These in turn allowed the chair to function in a broad range of commercial and domestic contexts ranging from stadium, office and auditorium to launderette, patio and kitchen table. This versatility was essential for the chair to be consumed in volumes that would justify its initial tooling investment. Combining low cost, elegant design and multiple end uses this chair was very successful. At the height of production the tool was capable of producing 4,000 seat shells per week, 14 million between 1963 and 2002. To date Day's Polyprop has been sold in over 20 countries worldwide, putting it (along with Thonet's No. 14)

among the most commercially successful chairs ever produced. Its success inevitably generated many even cheaper and formally poorer imitations but it has prevailed and is still in production today. The last and cheapest in a line of great shell chairs and the first and still the best of the plastic moulded variety.

Unearthing our particular buried specimen then was like revealing again in a very visceral way this ancestor and great, great, great, etc., grandfather to the multitude of generations of offspring. The idea of the 'ancestor' triggered an idea for the form of this chair.

In archaeologists' mode, similar polypropylene moulded shells that had been found were sorted and classified. Those which had an additional colour similarity to this Day original, were identified as having an attribute of family resemblance. These offspring would then be carried on the back of the original father.

stack of one

Stack of One (as shown on the front cover) was first called The Incomplete History of Stacking Chairs and is indeed assembled in ascending chronological order, starting with Landi chair, Hans Coray, 1938, at the base of the tower, followed by Antelope, Ernest Race, 1951, Seven chair, Arne Jacobsen, 1955, Polyprop, Robin Day, 1963, Selene, Vico Magisretti, 1969, and ending with Omkstack, Rodney Kinsman, 1972, at the top.

Clearly this is a stack selected from a much larger inventory of the genre. Others could be substituted and conceptually the stack is an infinite one. Each time a stack of this kind is constructed it will be a unique configuration, determined by both the order of the stack and the idiosyncratic, endlessly variable meeting of incongruous parts.

Stack of One is a paradox in name and form; a 'unique multiple' and a visual essay about form, function, the individual and the collective. These chairs all have a common rationale. They are each designed with the same functional requirement to stack and yet when brought together they do not fit with each other. This particular stack proves both that form does and does not follow function and that there is no such thing as consensus or an 'ideal'

functional form. A stacking chair by definition is always conceived as a collective item, something whose primary rational and formal resolution is determined by the 'idea' of acting in a replicated group. It is the very *raison d'etre* of this type of chair that it will never be a one off, yet specific examples of the genre are celebrated for their particularity. A delicious paradox of this type of chair is that each is in some way looked at and celebrated in its individual or unique cleverness in being able to perform very well with large numbers of its identical type. Individuality lies in the specific details of the formal resolution of the 'idea of stacking' and not somehow in the chair itself.

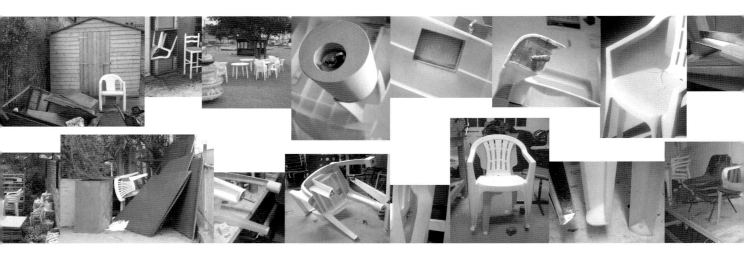

anonymous white
the ubiquitous white plastic stacking garden chair

plastic gold

The white plastic moulded outdoor chair is everywhere, all around the world. Everyone, at every level, sits on these chairs, somewhere. They have a kind of egalitarian ubiquity. From the sunny sides of exotic swimming pools, to suburban gardens, from allotment sheds and village halls to dusty, war-torn guerrilla out-posts; this chair is there.

It comes in various shapes and sizes, but somehow it is always the same – very cheap, very light and very anonymous. No one knows who designs these chairs. They are fantastically clever in their rationalised one piece injection moulded production and structure. They are paradoxically modest and pretentious. Basic, white and structurally pared down, yet simultaneously shaped like the thrones, basket chairs and wood carved seats from previous centuries. Most of all they are just there, in the generalised background, used and ignored, like air and pavements.

These chairs are very cheap and they declare it through their shiny flimsiness and candyfloss weight. They declare it by their one material uniformity. Level step changes in the surface, holes and cut outs attempt to disrupt the bland uniformity of material and surface. These elements hint at, but never deliver, the richness of multi-material fabrication and connection/detail construction. To buy a chair that is this cheap is to ignore or dismiss its pretensions; to use and abuse it without respect.

Considering these issues what is needed is a way to release these pretensions... to make them legitimate and to make the chair visible. To make it noticed for all of its aspirational aching to be more than ordinarily ordinary. This led to thinking about inversions and reversals. This is a crudely robust chair. How could it become fragile and delicate? It is uniformly monotonous with a mechanical poverty of surface and detail. How can it be invested with personality, with crafted idiosyncrasy? This is the cheapest of chairs. How could this be reversed and made valuable: the most expensive? This last is a problem of alchemy, of turning base material into gold. Gold was the trigger and experiments began in covering the chair with gold leaf.

On seeing the final chair many people asked why not simply spray the chair with gold paint? Wouldn't that be a whole lot quicker and easier to do? Well, yes it would, but we specifically and deliberately chose not to do that, because that is a cheap, theatrical trick and one where form does not follow idea in anything other than a very superficial way. The chair is not really transformed precisely because 'spray on' is quick and easy. It is part of the continuum of production that the chair already inhabits. Sprayed on gold paint changes the surface in a very uniform and mechanical way. It is a consistently superficial addition not a transformation. It changes it in a way that mirrors the mechanical injection moulded process that has been used to generate the chair in the first place; smooth and pre-determined.

Instead, the method employed here is a labour intensive, expensive theatrical trick. To hand lay gold

leaf on all of the surfaces of this chair takes time, patience and a great deal of skill. All the surfaces means exactly what it says; behind the back, under the armrests and beneath the seat. The chair is completely encased in a new skin of gold leaf. In the process the chair becomes more valuable both literally and symbolically. This is, from our point of view, what makes all the difference to the integrity, legitimacy and irony of the idea. It takes much more effort and care to produce this effect and the results of this strategy can be perceived in a number of ways. The tiling of the panels of gold leaf can be clearly seen and there is a difference to the quality of the shine in the surface. It is more fragmented and faceted. The vulnerable delicacy of the film of gold can be read. As a result, it is a chair that has to be responded to with consideration and respect precisely because it declares its delicacy. Without careful handling the gold may be broken, worn away on impatient thumbs or lost in careless fingernails. Here we are facing the possibility of a reversal of the Midas touch. If we are not careful we will turn gold back into plastic.

And gold: it's that stuff! Not just gold but gold on a scale as large as a chair! People are compelled to touch it; they just cannot help themselves. When this chair was first exhibited at the Solone del Mobile in Milan people registered a kind of amused and shocked disbelief of dual recognition. They were expecting chairs. They were walking through the vast halls of an exhibition centre, which, in that week, held chairs by the acre. This though was a chair that should not be in these particular halls of discriminating design. They knew the chair; it was that chair from everywhere. They knew gold, that ancient and untarnishable god, and they were faced with a kind of incongruous but somehow entirely reasonable marriage of opposites. It seems so wrong and yet it seems so right. Normally these chairs have formal pretensions above their station. Everyone knows this but usually looks the other way, embarrassed at the pretence (that is why they are invisible), but at that price how can you resist if you keep your eyes half closed? Now here was the chair in its rightful garb, in its always-promised inheritance. Cloaked in a kind of fabulous, honest dishonesty. A garb that has always been latent if only it could just try it on and convince us. How can you not want to touch and admire the peacock audacity of it!

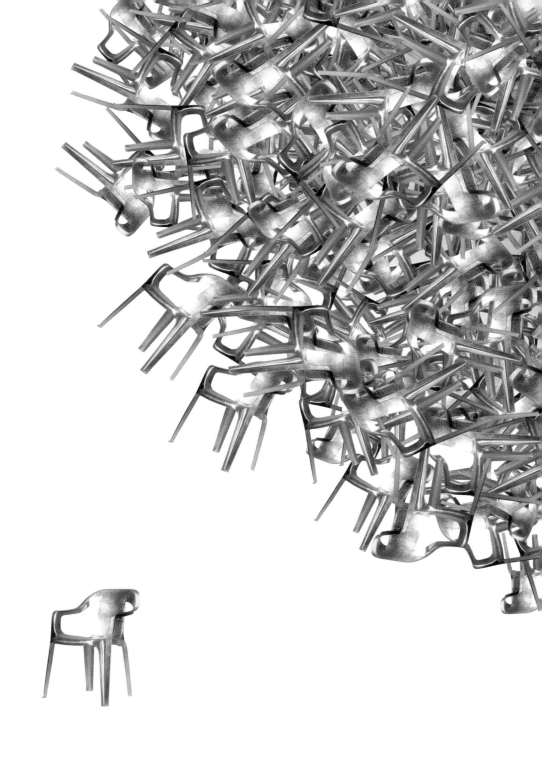

co-dependent

This chair is made from two chairs; one for the price of two. But the two are mutually supportive – one could not live without the other. Literally, conceptually and historically there are several reversals in this dual chair idea, which give it additional resonance and irony.

First, there is the parallel coincidence regarding the condition of the chairs when they were found in different places. The first find was the 'anonymous white' found at the top of a hill of domestic housing, fallen next to a wall, next to a bin. Waiting to be dragged off by the refuse collectors and fed into the metal jaws of the iron stomached refuse truck which re-consumes everything that we have previously consumed and have now rejected. The chair was waiting for this fate, fallen because one of its back legs was missing. An all round search, including a tentative but sufficiently thorough examination of the contents of the adjacent bin, failed to uncover the missing leg. Easy to imagine (in this metaphorical archaeology) that the separated leg, in grubby bone white, had been carried off by a wolf or dog. The rest of the chair was rescued without yet knowing what to do with it. At this stage it was a random find disconnected by thought or form to any idea. It was simply collected because it was one of

the types of invisible chairs identified for release from their invisibility.

It is an interesting phenomenon that starting a process often attracts immediate sensitivity to other relevant material. Once focused on the dig, once saturated in the mental terrain of a specific exploration, coincidences always line up to present themselves.

Thus another chair was found, again quite by accident, while walking through a basement car park. It was fallen alongside bin bags full of the also discarded. This chair also had a back leg missing. Similarly this leg could not be found despite an equally enterprising reconnaissance of the bin liners nearby. The first chair was the anonymous white but this second one was a chair of more prominent, cultural visibility. It was a Wait chair designed by Matthew Hilton and produced by Authentics. However, in addition to the coincidence of the broken legs, both of these chairs were of the same general type formally and structurally. Chairs formed from one single continuous moulded shell-like piece of plastic, cleverly configured to deliver structural rigidity by use of angle section legs and integral stiffening ribs. The type of which there are now

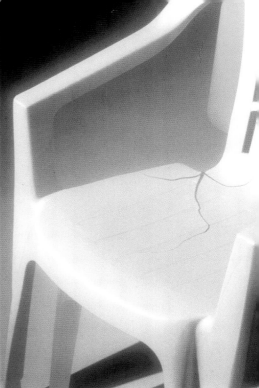

many variations, representing the realisation of one idealised route for mass-produced chairs: single moulding, stacking with four integral legs. This was originally a difficult feat to pull off structurally. It was first achieved by a state of the art, design led manufacturer who was prepared to put in serious investment and time to push the boundaries and go where no chair had gone before. The integral legged, single moulded chair represents one of the landmarks of chair production in the twentieth century, and one of the first chairs to achieve this was the Selene chair by Vico Magistretti, produced by Artemide in 1969.

Anonymous white had its back right leg missing; Hilton's Wait chair had its back left leg missing. Brought together they had a complete set of back legs. Although one was common and the other aristocratic they were cousins of a collective ancestry. This suggests that there should be some formal compatibility in mutual support. Also it is usually the case that the high design chair breaks new ground and comes before its cheaper imitators, the first one supporting the development of the other. Although physically newer the Hilton chair has the aristocratic heritage and should represent the thoroughbred culture from which other variations modestly model themselves. So the co-dependent chair was constructed with the Hilton below representing authentic original and the white on top as subsequent copy. A modified copy is sometimes also referred to as a cover version. In formal terms here the ubiquitous white literally 'covers' the 'authentic' Hilton chair. Here there are word games, puns and associations informing and defining the realisation of this object. Clearly words are important here, but as an example of shorthand invention and support, not as an elaborately contrived, excessively long substitution.

office chairs

24 star

The secretarial office chair is another generic type, with its single metal stalk growing from a root like base. This base type started life as a reduced form of pedestal or tripod construction. Flattening the tripod, bringing the apex of a tripod down near to the ground and combining this with the cantilever principle employed by earlier chairs produces a kind of radial cantilever with the vertical element in the centre. The seat of the chair sits centrally above the resulting single upright support column.

Later additions to this basic principle allowed the chair seat and back to swivel independently of its base and for the seat height and tilt to be adjusted. A tripod like structure is a stable support for something immediately and statically above its apex. However this stability is compromised when the load above is spread irregularly outside of the triangular base and the centre of gravity is dynamic. A seated person presents both of these conditions and it follows that three legged seats although structurally

viable are prone to overbalance under a dynamic load and apart from very low stools have never been predominant on the furniture landscape. Bases with four radiating foot elements became the norm for office chairs until the 1980s.

When Frank Lloyd Wright designed the Johnson Wax Building in Racine, Wisconsin he also designed all of its original furniture including a three-legged secretarial chair. This chair is unstable and will tip over if the 'correct' posture is not assumed. Anecdotally it is reported that when someone suggested to Wright that secretaries would fall off the chair he is reputed to have replied that "they will only do it once". True or false this form of dismissive arrogance is no longer possible and the design of office chairs has become subject to specific safety standards. In the early 1980s successive safety testing established that the so called 'four star' base configuration still had the potential to overbalance and that the provision of

five radial foot elements was to be the optimum and definitive standard. 'Five star' bases where born to ensure operational stability for all chairs with this type of central pedestal base which are designed for use in the commercial and public sectors.

Whole constellations of five star chairs are now predominant, clustering the firmament of commercial office space; their very ubiquity rendering them invisible as idiosyncratic individuals, as they become lost in an expanding galaxy of other five stars. While five stars are outshining each other in self cancelling glare, four stars are a dying breed simply because they are no longer made and previous generations are dying in scrap heaps or lost in dim clusters in the backs of second hand furniture stores. The 'red dwarfs' of the office chair genre, four stars are about to become extinct.

24 Star presents the rescue and reinstatement of a dying four star from this fate. Here this chair is

provided with excessive insurance that it will not fall over; the potentially unstable is made massively and reassuringly stable. At the end of each four star foot a five star base is added. The original four points of ground contact are transformed and spread out into 20 points of contact covering a much wider footprint. The chair floats on a raft of 20 outspread castors. Sitting in the centre of this commingling lattice it is impossible to tip it over. If the office worker falls off this one it will his/her own fault. Red dwarf is revived and expands to become blue giant.

starbase

This is a reconstruction that celebrates the current
dominance and growth of the five star office
chair, the rise of whose bases are compared and
contrasted as generations which root and sprout.
These bases are all the same and all different
and are variously made from pressed steel, cast
aluminium or injection moulded plastic. This is a
super dense column constructed to reveal variety in
both material and shape. Starbase is a highly visible
expression of the diversity within uniformity of this
type of chair base and an exposure of its relative
invisibility. Starbase also uncovers the large range of
castors, which provide, taken for granted, ease and
versatility of movement. Castors operate as silent
miracles of engineering beneath our seats. Here they
are revealed as satellites held at the ends of the
stars influence and explicitly illustrate their normally
invisible, spinning and revolving, circular orbit
around the central column.

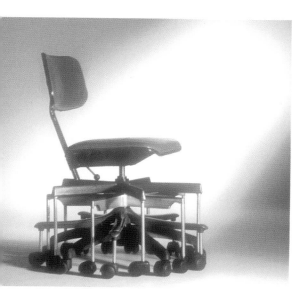

glossary

In the introduction to this book we coined the ironic axiom "absolutes they come and they go". We take the view that not all facts or definitions are stable, some are permeable and are subject to cultural revision, reinterpretation and redefinition. What was a fact for Newton was not a fact for Einstein. Relativity tells us that truth depends on the position from which you view it and that the observer cannot be detached from the observed. In keeping with the subjective, poetic, rhetorical and non-literary position taken with the text, imagery and spirit of this book, the glossary below is a selective account of terms, concepts, people and things that have informed and reflect our particular way of thinking and designing.

artists, designers, theorists, manufacturers

Adams, Ansel, 1902-84
San Francisco-born photographer and conservationist, best known for his landscapes of the American west.

Adams, Scott, 1957-
American cartoonist, creator of the Dilbert comic strip.

Anderson, Laurie, 1947-
Visual and performance artist, musician, and theatre practitioner.

Artemide
Italian manufacturers best known for lighting design (qv. Magistretti).

Authentics
German design brand which since the 1990s has focused upon plastics. The characteristically simple lines of their design were established by artist Johannes Maier in the first half of the twentieth century. Wait chair, designed by Matthew Hilton, is produced by this company.

Ball, Keith, 1955-
Artist, exhibited widely in London, Moscow, New York, Stockholm. Founded The Commercial Gallery in 1995, an artist-run space in Spitalfields, London, and "Commercial Too", a series of large-scale offsite exhibitions in temporary unused office and warehouse spaces. Co-curated the Whitechapel Open 96 with Richard Wentworth and Alison Wilding.
Studioball set up in 2000 with Maxine Naylor Ball and Ralph Ball.

Baudrillard, Jean, 1929-
French cultural theorist, whose works include the seminal essay "The Precession of Simulacra", first published in English in *Simulations*, 1983. Baudrillard's writings have helped to define the concepts of post structuralism and the Postmodern. He argues that contemporary media, consumption and production structures have displaced reality and given rise to a 'hyperreal' condition, in which the possibility of genuine origin is lost.

Bauhaus
One of the most influential movements of twentieth century design, Bauhaus was an art school founded by Walter Gropius (qv.) in Germany, in 1919, advocating a fundamentalist aesthetic and geometrically pure form.

Bey, Jurgen, 1965-
Dutch designer whose playful designs utilise found objects (qv. Droog).

Brancusi, Constantin, 1876-1957
Romanian abstract sculptor, whose doctrine of "truth to materials" – that is, leaving the artistic material as much as possible in its natural state – was an important influence on mid-twentieth century modernist art and design.

Branzi, Andrea, 1938-
Architect, designer, academic and theoretician, based in Milan, and much involved with radical Italian architecture from the 1960s on. A key figure and participant in both Studio Alchimia, 1976, and Memphis, 1981 (qv.), provocative design groups which challenged the status quo of mainstream rational design.

Calder, Alexander, 1898-1976
American sculptor, painter and designer best known for his 'mobiles', hanging sculptures in painted steel whose components float and drift in seemingly arbitrary and lyrical response to small changes in air current.

Coray, Hans, 1906-91
Swiss designer and artist, best known for the Landi Chair, 1938. Coray's design won a competition for outdoor seating for the Schweizerische Landesaustellung (Swiss National Exhibition, Zurich, 1939). The chair takes its name from its strong association with the exhibition. Its form and production used the latest developments in both material alloys and hardening methods. The first successful production model was made entirely from aluminium and weighed only three kilos.

Dali, Salvador, 1904-89
Spanish artist and self-styled eccentric, prominent twentieth century personality, associated with the Surrealist movement.

Day, Robin, 1915-
British designer best known for his Polyprop stacking chair, the first chair design to fully exploit injection moulding as a mass manufacturing process (qv. injection moulding, polypropylene).

Droog Design
Dutch design collective established in 1993 by design historian Renny Ramakers and designer Gijs Bakker; 'Droog' translates as 'dry', with reference to the humour that informs their work (qv. Jurgen Bey, Hella Jongerius, Marcel Wanders, who have all been associated with Droog).

Duchamp, Marcel, 1887-1968
French artist, involved with the Surrealist movement; the door he designed for 11 Rue Larrey is a typical example of his conceptually provocative and enigmatic approach.

Eames, Charles, 1907-78
Designer who, with his wife Ray, produced furniture, buildings, toys, games, and films, including the influential *Powers of Ten*, 1968.

Escher, MC, 1898-1972
Dutch graphic artist most famous for his 'impossible structures' and distortions of perspective, and complex tessellations.

Fehlbaum, Rolf, 1941-
Chief executive of Swiss furniture design company Vitra, owners of a large portion of the Eames estate (qv.).

Frayling, Christopher, 1946-
Rector of the Royal College of Art and Chair of the Arts Council of England; historian, critic and broadcaster, knighted in 1991.

Gropius, Walter, 1883-1969
German founder of the Bauhaus (qv.). Gropius coined the Bauhaus dictum "starting from zero", aspiring to a pure socialist approach and rejecting all historical baggage.

Hilton, Matthew, 1957-
British designer whose stacking Wait Chair for Authentics is made from fully recyclable plastic, and aims at democratic pricing and design.

Jacobsen, Arne, 1902-71
Hugely influential Danish architect and designer, whose Series Seven Chair, 1955, was one of the most popular and enduring chair designs of the last 50 years.

Jongerius, Hella, 1963-
Rotterdam-based designer who combines her background in industrial design with traditional craft influences (qv. Droog).

Kinsman, Rodney, 1943-
Chairman and Managing Director of London-based OMK Design; his Omkstack Chair, 1972, in metal and chrome epitomised the high-tech functionality of 1970s design.

Koestler, Arthur, 1905-83
Hungarian-born British journalist, novelist and critic. A politically active author, he spoke against totalitarianism in Eastern Europe; his later career focused on questions of telepathy and extra-sensory perception. *The Act of Creation*, 1964, is the second in a trilogy of books by Koestler investigating the phenomenon of 'mind' and culminating in *The Ghost in the Machine*, published in 1967.

Leipzig, Arthur, 1918-
Esteemed New York photographer, and Professor of Long Island University. Edward Steichen included his work in the controversial, landmark exhibition "Family of Man" at the Museum of Modern Art, 1955. Leipzig's urban photography is in the tradition of the street photographer, capturing the daily life of New York in the middle of the twentieth century.

Lessing, Erich, 1884-1959
One of Magnum's first photographers, noted for his post-war work in which he documented both the devastation of Europe, and its artistic resurgence through a series of portraits of actors, dancers, artists, directors and musicians.

Lock, Andrew, 1969-
Visual artist working with photography. Although they function at one level as documents of specific, typically prosaic and often marginal locations, Andrew Lock's images are also an attempt to explore the social and psychological significance of these sites. To this end, his treatment of subjects commonly exhibits a complexity that belies their apparently trivial status and invests them with a compelling sense of drama.

Loos, Adolph, 1870-1933
Vienna-based architect, whose essay "Ornament and Crime" expressed his opposition to the Art Nouveau movement in favour of a rational, undecorative approach, espousing simple, functional design.

Madoz, Chema, 1958-
Based in Spain, Madoz is among the country's most prominent art photographers. His simply staged, black and white images record the sculptures he makes from everyday objects, repositioned and combined so as to make the viewer re-examine the familiar.

Magistretti, Vico, 1920-
Milanese architect and designer, committed to producing simple but elegant objects for mass production; the moulded plastic Selene Chair, from 1969, is a case in point.

Memphis
Seminal 'Postmodern' Milan-based design collective formed in the 1980s, led by veteran Italian architect Ettore Sottsass.

Munari, Bruno, 1907-98
Italian artist, writer, architect, designer and philosopher. Munari was associated with the Futurist movement, which celebrated the aesthetic of the machine and the dynamic fluidity of modern life. He was specifically interested in re-framing the possibilities of that which is already around us, rather than the conventional modernist position of "starting from zero". In this sense his work took an inclusive rather than an exclusive position.

Noguchi, Isamu, 1904-88
American designer and sculptor best known for the IN50 glass topped coffee table, mass produced by Herman Miller from 1944, and for his Akari paper light range, 1944 and 1951-56. In addition to design he produced a prolific body of sculpture primarily using stone, exploiting with restrained elegance the simple monumental presence of material and surface.

Picasso, Pablo, 1881-1973
Spanish artist and sculptor, one of the definitive figures of twentieth century art.

Race, Ernest, 1913-64
Leading post-war designer of functional, economic furniture, mass produced for use in public and private spaces. His durable Antelope Chair was widely used on the South Bank during the Festival of Britain in 1951.

Rietveld, Gerrit, 1888-1964
Danish architect and designer, whose Red Blue Chair of 1917 was radical in its abstract and reductive approach to the formal requirements of a chair. The chair is iconic and has had a lasting impact as a classic of modernist design.

van der Rohe, Ludwig Mies, 1886-1969
Director of the Bauhaus (qv.), his mantra "less is more" epitomises modernist aesthetics. He sought a universal architecture based on simple line, and structural and material integrity.

SITE
James Wines' (qv.) architecture firm (Sculpture in the Environment). SITE argue and express through their work that architecture should integrate narrative and psychological dimensions to provide a rich, multi-layered experience in engaging with the built environment. Best Products Co. Inc. commissioned a series of seven showrooms in the 1970s, which included *Tilt*, Towson, Maryland, 1978, *Notch*, Sacramento, California, 1977, and *Indeterminate Facade*, Houston, Texas, 1975, each a challenge to the standard box structures of commercial space.

Sullivan, Louis, 1856-1924
Among America's most influential architects, Sullivan rejected historical precedent in favour of an approach which addressed the functional requirements of each individual project, as well as the materials and technologies available at the time – hence the famous dictum "form follows function".

Thonet, Michael, 1796-1871
Vienna-based maker of bent-wood furniture; he patented the process in England, France and Belgium. A pioneer of mass manufacture, 15 million of his No. 14 Chair, developed in 1859, had been produced by 1893.

Venturi, Robert, 1925-
American architect and author whose 1966 book *Complexity and Contradiction in Modern Architecture* challenged the dictates of modernism and argued for an architecture which engaged with human use, the contextual ambiguities and contradictions of the city. The equally influential *Learning from Las Vegas*, published in 1972, developed his theories on urban sprawl and the strip mall, the culture of the big sign and the highway (qv. Postmodernism).

Wanders, Marcel, 1963-
Dutch designer with a background in industrial design; became known in the mid 1990s for his innovative Knotted Chair, which was taken on by Italian manufacturers Cappellini. Worked with Droog before setting up his own studio, Moooi.

Wines, James, 1932-
American architect whose designs made a significant impact on the 1970s; rejecting the industrialism of modernism, he favours an environmentally conscious approach to design (qv. SITE).

Wright, Frank Lloyd, 1867-1959
American architect, designer and theorist. Wright exerted an enormous influence on the decorative arts and became known as one of the greatest American architects. His work was crucial to the development of architectural practice in the twentieth century and had a great influence on the embryonic development of modern design in Europe. Wright believed that the furniture of a house should reflect the entire structure and designed furniture for most of his own buildings.

terms, concepts and technologies

abstract
An essence or ideal; a theoretical way of regarding things associated with Modernist aesthetics, which reduces phenomena to their most fundamental expression in diagram or symbol. In art, design and architectural terms this represented a search for a universal inventory of shapes and forms supposedly to be culturally neutral, devoid of any vernacular, allegorical or partisan cultural reading and to exhibit a 'pure' aesthetic.

academic practice
Concerned primarily with the development and culture of ideas, often independently of their specific commercial value or potential. The pursuit of knowledge for its own sake. The term academic is derived from the 'academy' originally the garden near Athens where Plato taught and subsequently meaning a place of study and scholarly pursuit and relating quite specifically to education.

anonymous white
Ball and Naylor's term for the generic and ubiquitous one piece white plastic stacking chair, designed for outdoor use.

archaeology
Literally the study of ancient things; the term archaeology has developed and grown to embrace a much wider set of meanings through common usage as the discipline itself has expanded and matured. The American archaeologist Walter Taylor (1913-97) writing in 1948 was confidently able to assert that: "Archaeology is neither history nor anthropology. As an autonomous discipline, it consists of a method and a set of specialised techniques for the gathering or 'production' of cultural information."

archaeology of the invisible
This term is used by Ball and Naylor to describe their approach to design, recovering that which has become metaphorically buried in contemporary living by reinvention – see 'anonymous white' above and its rebirth in Plastic Gold and Co-dependent.

axiom
An established principle or maxim; a rule of conduct that in part defines the parameters of a particular discipline. A general, self evident truth.

Cartesian co-ordinates
These are height, width, and depth, the so-called x, y and z directions of three-dimensional space. By use of these three any point can be located and any shape mapped. The term derives from the original mathematical writings of René Descartes in his famous work "Discourse on the Method of Properly Guiding the Reason in the Search for Truth", 1637. Descartes founded the premise that the entire world can be described mathematically and understood by logic and reason. This rational approach to defining the world was adopted and reinterpreted visually by early pioneers of modernism in art and design including Rietvelt, de Stijl, the Constructivists, and the Bauhaus (qv.).

concept
An idea, thought, or notion conceived through mental activity. The words concept and conception are applied to mental formulations on a broad scale.

conceptual
In general, referring to concepts or conception. In reference to art, imagery that departs from perceived accuracy to present a mental formulation of the object, rather than its appearance alone.

Conceptual art is intended to convey an idea or a concept to the perceiver, rejecting the creation or appreciation of a traditional art object, such as a painting or a sculpture, as a precious commodity. The idea is the most important aspect of the work. All planning and decisions are made before hand, and the execution is a secondary act.

creative practice
Engaging in the process of generating new ideas, interpretations, solutions, images or forms. A stage-by-stage outline of this process usually involves the following:

Finding or formulating a problem. The American psychologist George Kneller called this stage "first insight". Researching and drawing from life experiences (memory), networking, etc.. This stage is variously called "discovery" or "saturation".

Mulling over the problem in a chaos of ideas and knowledge, letting go of certainties (forgetting). Another American psychologist, Jacob Getzel, called this stage "incubation" – engaging the intuitive, non-sequential, or global thinking at the core of creativity.

One or more ideas surface. This is also called "immersion" and "illumination".

The idea is tested as a potential solution to the problem. Getzel called this "verification". This final stage often involves "revision" – conscious structuring and editing of created material.

creativity

One of the fundamentals of Art and Design practice and yet one which, comes under pressure when time constraints predominate. In these situations it becomes easier to default to the formulaic and the systematised. As design matures it tends to pull in implicit formal rules and the more expediently these are applied the more generic and uniform the visual output becomes (qv. Neo-Modernism).

Even in the creative industries it is easy to fall in line with our own rules. Generally, creativity is hampered by the 'rules' we think we are supposed to operate by: be logical, don't be messy, be structured, get it right. The very concept of rules is pretty much antithetical to the creative process and yet we let them constrict us and limit what we allow ourselves to do creatively.

Creativity comes from laying aside the rules – even for just a little while – so that we are able to reach beyond logic and structure and tap into our imaginations more easily. This is the place where we store our sense of the ridiculous, our sense of being able to do the impossible

and ultimately, our ability to see things differently and find new and usable solutions.

design rules

Implicit set of received opinions constituting the operational parameters of the design discipline. For example Modernist axioms such as "less is more", "form follows function", "truth to materials", etc., when taken together form an implicit code of practice. As with all rules, used with critical flexibility and maturity as a guide or reference, they can deliver elegant optimisation; used without such reflection they can quickly turn to formulaic and witless dogma.

Esperanto

'Dr Esperanto' (meaning 'one who hopes') was the pseudonym of Dr LL Zamenhof, 1859-1917, who in 1887 published a language designed to function as a universal means of communication between nations and peoples. The language, which became known by its creator's *nom de plume*, borrows from and combines a number of existing languages, and is designed to be easily learned and spoken.

furniture

The movable contents of a house or room, typically taken to refer to tables, chairs, beds and storage units. Furniture more properly includes the increasingly diverse range of objects that populate our interior spaces. Furniture may also refer to the smaller elements which articulate urban landscapes, for example traffic and street lighting, post boxes, road signs, refuse bins, bus stops, and so on.

genre

Form of categorisation, in which objects or works are grouped according to shared similarities in particular type or style.

injection moulding

Industrial process of injecting molten plastic polymer into a desired mould. Although initial tools investment is high, the process renders a very low unit production cost and, owing to this economic viability, is the most common form of mass production in plastics manufacture. Polypropylene (qv.), the plastic most often used in mass chair manufacture, was first injection moulded for this purpose in 1963. (qv. Robin Day, Polyprop).

integrated seat/back shell chair
Chair in which the seat and back is made from one continuous piece of moulded material. Experiments in this form started in earnest in the 1930s, as designers sought a model for economical mass production. The advent of injection moulding (qv.) as a viable process allowed this model to dominate.

intuition
David G Myers, in his book *Intuition: Its Powers and Perils*, 2002, demonstrates through numerous well-replicated experiments that intuition − "our capacity for direct knowledge, for immediate insight without observation or reason" − is as much a component of our thinking as analytical logic.

Intuition is not subliminal perception; it is subtle perception and learning − knowing without knowing that you know. Intellect and intuition are complementary, not competitive. Without intellect, our intuition may drive us unchecked into emotional chaos. Without intuition, we risk failing to resolve complex social dynamics and moral dilemmas.

irrational
Apparently unreasonable, illogical and absurd, not commensurable with recognised and familiar patterns.

mass production
Any industrial process based on rapid, economic, bulk manufacture of a product, as opposed to small-scale or individual construction, resulting in a series of identical objects. The development of mass production techniques in the twentieth century was key to the advent of modern consumer society, as simple, functional design became available to all (qv. Jean Baudrillard).

mature and immature object types
In Ball and Naylor's terms, 'mature object types' are those which have become 'culturally embedded'; a 'consistent base form' (such as table, chair, bowl) underlies variations of use and design. 'Immature object types' are those which, owing to rapid shifts in technology, do not settle into a base form, although the function remains the same − for example, the telephone.

methodology
A specified procedure or approach, usually in an organised and orderly fashion. Methodologies can alternatively be constructed which deliberately set out to disrupt the step-by-step linear process. Brain storming and lateral thinking are examples (qv. problem solving: lateral thinking and Edward de Bono).

Modernism
Broadly, Modernism originated in the 1880s; the term covers a diverse range of schools, practices and movements across the arts, loosely united by a drive to move away from historical styles and invent new forms, a shift in part stimulated by advances in industrial process and the advance of the machine age. In architecture and design, as a periodising term 'Modernism' applies as much to art nouveau as it does to minimalism. However, in common usage 'Modernist' describes design that reaches towards clean lines, functionalism, simplicity, and structural integrity, ideals which dominated the middle of the twentieth century (qv. Bauhaus, Constantin Brancusi, Hans Coray, Robin Day, Charles Eames, Arne Jacobsen, Rodney Kinsman, Ernest Race, Gerrit Rietveld, Louis Sullivan, Ludwig Mies van der Rohe).

monism
Doctrine or theory that proclaims singularity of state or system, and denies the existence or value of dual or multiple positions or states.

multi-layered
Having more than one layer. In the context of design, this may refer to layers of meaning or interpretation as well as materials. In non safety-critical situations, the ambiguity of different interpretations can endow an object with endlessly renewable fascination.

Museum of Modern Art (MoMA)
Established in New York in 1929 to meet the need for a museum devoted exclusively to modern art, MoMA has occupied its 53rd Street building in Manhattan since 1939. The site closed in 2002 to allow for extensive renovations under the direction of Japanese architect Yoshio Taniguchi, reopening its doors late in 2004.

narrative

Story told or written usually through subjective observation, unfolding in a continuous account. In art and design terms, the same concept assigned and applied to an object, exhibition, or building. The notion of a surrounding or integral story or sequence of events is embedded within the design. For example the architectural work of SITE or Venturi and Rauch.

Neo-Modernism

A term which has emerged in the wake of Postmodernism (qv.) to describe a return to Modernist ideals of purity, abstraction, and formal reduction in a digital age. Often this return delivers poor facsimiles of previously established modern forms, rather than attempting to recast Modernist ideology in a more inventive and contemporary manner.

paradox

A statement, notion or proposition, literal, mathematical or visual, that apparently contradicts itself but by holding in place two opposing principles creates a kind of poetic truth in this impossible reconciliation. Something holding attractive fascination because of its indeterminate state (for example, the drawings of Escher (qv.), or the writings of Jorge Luis Borges).

Platonic solids

The Platonic solids belong to the group of geometric figures called polyhedra. A polyhedron is a three-dimensional solid bounded by plane polygons. The polygons are called faces; they intersect in edges; the points where three or more edges intersect are called vertices.

A regular polyhedron is one whose faces are identical regular polygons. Only five regular solids are possible: cube, tetrahedron, octahedron, icosahedron, and dodecahedron.

pluralistic

System that recognises more than one ultimate principle. Postmodernism (qv.) in design and architectural terms was a pluralistic, multi-stylistic reaction to the monism of Modernism (qv.), which came to dominate design culture in the mid-twentieth century.

poetic

In common usage, elevated expression of elevated thought. Transferred to design it refers to objects which are equally elevated above the pragmatic and formal requirement of the functional artefact, and deliver ambient observations in condensed form for reflection and contemplation. Like literary poetry, poetic design requires that to focus such observations poignantly, some of the normal constraints of functional pragmatism may be deliberately or selectively distorted or suspended.

poetics of the everyday

Ball and Naylor's term to describe a celebration of ordinary, commonly used objects by a process of re-evaluation, re-framing and reconstruction. These acts aim to create 'poetic resonance'; a renewed awareness, appreciation and re-valuing of that which is already so much established as to have become culturally invisible.

polypropylene

A versatile vinyl polymer used in a wide range of product industries, as both a plastic and a fibre. It has a high melting point, is easy to dye, and is water-resistant, making it an ideal material for economical mass production (qv. Robin Day, Polyprop).

Pop

Pop Art originated in 1950s Britain, but came to prominence in New York in the 1960s under the auspices, most famously, of Andy Warhol. Pop Art turned to popular culture and daily life, media, advertising, and mass production, as a source of inspiration, celebrating consumer culture and eroding the perceived gap between 'high' and 'low' art.

Postmodernism

As widely-used and diversely-defined a term as you could hope to find, applied across disciplines from sociology to technology to art theory. In design terms, it can be loosely understood as a movement in the late twentieth century away from the formalism and purity that Modernism represents. While Modernism seeks to find universal structures, Postmodernism reasserts context and seeks to retrieve the ambiguities and complexities of everyday life. Designers and architects who are described as 'Postmodern' often meet this challenge with witty, parodic responses, reclaiming histories and mixing cultural referents (qv. Droog, Memphis, Constantin Venturi, Andrea Branzi).

post-rationalism

A way of thinking, typifying Postmodern (qv.) theory, which accepts ideas, ideologies and philosophies as intellectual tools rather than truths; also trusting to processes beyond the rational, such as instinct, association and coincidence.

Kierkegaard said that "Life must be understood backwards, but lived forwards." Real human enterprises succeed or fail through subjective, chaotic, irrational behaviour. Management gurus proclaiming revolution and paradigm shifts consistently emphasise this (such as Malcolm Gladwell, in the recent *Blink: The Power of Thinking Without Thinking*, 2005), whilst enterprise information models which continue to rely solely on scientific rationale conspire to misinform.

problem solving

logical problem solving

runs through procedural checklists; for example:
Look at the problem.
Have you seen a similar problem before?
If so, how is this problem similar? How is it different?
What facts do you have?
What do you know that is not stated in the problem?
How have you solved similar problems in the past?
What strategies do you know?
Try a strategy that seems as if it will work.
If it doesn't, it may lead you to one that will.
Use the strategy you selected and work the problem.
Reread the question.
Did you answer the question asked?
Does your answer seem reasonable?

lateral thinking

Edward de Bono has written extensively about the process of what he calls lateral thinking—the generation of novel solutions to problems. The point of lateral thinking is that many problems require a different perspective to solve successfully. De Bono identifies four critical factors associated with lateral thinking: 1 recognise dominant ideas that polarise perception of a problem, 2 searching for different ways of looking at things, 3 relaxation of rigid control of thinking, and 4 use of chance to encourage other ideas. This last factor has to do with the fact that lateral thinking involves low-probability ideas, which are unlikely to occur in the normal course of events.

rational

Conforming to that which seems reasonable and concerned with that which can be proved by quantifiable facts.

reflective

In conceptual and theoretical design terms, concerned with reviewing in thought what has been uncovered in practice. Meditation or consultation with oneself about process, results and implications.

rhetoric

The art of persuasive speaking or writing; the use of argumentative devices and artificial or extravagant language to persuade or impress. A rhetorical question is one that does not require an answer but is employed to make apparent that the only possible answer is a given. Transferred to design the same operations using selective visual language may be deployed to make particularly focused points through object or image.

theoretical

Concerned with knowledge but not with its practical application. Speculative, but not dealing directly with facts and objects as presented by direct experience.

theory

Collections and extrapolations of results designed to illustrate principles of a subject, most commonly delivered in written or numeric form. A way of explaining something based on principles independent of the phenomenon to be explained.

Victoria & Albert Museum

West London museum for the applied and decorative arts. Established as the South Kensington Museum in 1852 following the success of the Great Exhibition, 1951, and renamed in honour of the Queen and her late consort in 1899. Holds much of the culturally defined important examples of material culture, across typologies and historic periods up to the present day.

visual bibliography

Analogous to literary bibliography: a source of visual reference, which informs the current visual output of the authors. Ambience, quality of light, texture, materiality, manifestations of the sensations of mass, lightness, cultural association, formal similarities, conceptual correspondences, links to other objects, stories and formal analogies.

visual research
Finding, responding to and manipulating visual material.
Finding can be by any means and implies being alert to the
accidental, asking what information does this or that object,
texture, colour, or form reveal or imply. How can it be used,
modified, put together with other material and what
interpretations do these further combinations suggest?

visual vocabulary; visual dialogue/discourse
Analogous to literary units such as nouns, adjectives,
verbs, adverbs, sentences and paragraphs. Visual
vocabulary is the use of visual components such as dot,
line, plane, volume, colour, surface, material, texture,
light and shadow, the use of culturally understood symbols
and sub-assemblies; the use of visual metaphors.

Vitra Design Museum
The Vitra Design Museum in Weil am Rhein opened in
1989; it is associated with, but financially independent
from, the Vitra Design Company. This museum holds
originals of the most important and influential chairs
designed from mid nineteenth century to the present.
The museum was founded on the personal furniture
collection of Rolf Fehlbaum, CEO of Vitra (qv.).

wallpaper*
International design and lifestyle magazine launched
in 1996. Its content is entirely aspirational and escapist,
its models fabulously thin and beautiful, its interiors
immaculate and vast. Its ethos: the consumption of
superficial image, not content.

zeitgeist
From the German, the spirit of the time (literally,
'zeit' meaning time and 'geist' meaning ghost); the
characteristic intellectual and cultural outlook of a
specific place and time.

credits and acknowledgments

Unless otherwise identified all objects, graphic images and sketch drawings are the work of Maxine Naylor and/or Ralph Ball.

pp. 52, 61, 61, 63, 64, 71, 81 (bottom middle, bottom right), 89, 90, 103, 107 photography David Spero
p. 64 (right) photography Richard Davies
pp. 14, 15, 16, 32 (bottom), 34, 37, 39, 49, 50, 51, 60 (bottom), 67, 68, 69, 72, 73 (top), 88, 91, 94, 97, 102, 103, 104, 105, 106 photography Maxine Naylor
pp. 17, 28, 43, 57, 60, (top, middle), 73 (bottom), 92, 95, 96 photography Ralph Ball
p. 80 photography Ori Gersht
pp. 35, 55, 59, 81 (bottom left) Chema Madoz
p. 6 from *Chinese Acrobatics*, Beijing: Foreign Languages Press, 1981
p. 7 © Neil Dawson 1993
p. 8 © Jerry N. Uelsmann 2001
p. 10 © Michael Wolf/Katz Pictures
p. 12 from *Observer Magazine*, 19 July 1970
pp. 20, 21, 32 (top) © Andy Lock 2003
p. 25 photography Chris Toby
p. 29 © Theo Ball 2004
pp. 44, 45 photographs of *Powers of Ten a Flipbook*
p. 52 © Keith Ball 1993
p. 74 © akg-images/Erich Lessing
p. 75 © Arthur Leipzig
p. 77 © Succession Marcel Duchamp/ADAGP, Paris and DACS, London 2005
pp. 78, 82, 83, 85 © SITE

The Archaeology of the Invisible collection was developed under the authors' research project 'Sustaining Desire, the chair as cultural, visual and ecological narrative', with the aid of an Innovation Award from the Arts and Humanities Research Board (AHRB), with additional development work supported by the Faculty of Art Architecture and Design, University of Lincoln and Central Saint Martins College of Art and Design.

For various forms of help, advice or encouragement the authors would like to thank Max Ball, Theo Ball, Dr Kate Fletcher, Ingo Maurer, Valerie Naylor, Robert Pulley, and Dr Mirjam Southwell. Additionally Stephen Dalby, research assistant on 'Sustaining Desire', and all at Black Dog Publishing for their energy, effort and commitment, with particular thanks to Emilia Gómez López, Amy Sackville and Duncan McCorquodale for help, advice and patience beyond the call of duty.

biographies

Professor Maxine Naylor

Maxine Naylor is a furniture and lighting designer, and Professor of Design at the University of Lincoln. Her award-winning and influential design work has been exhibited widely in the United Kingdom, United States and Europe. Naylor has won design awards from the Industrial Designers Society of America (IDSA); the Best Lamp Award from Table Lamp and Chair in the USA; and has received a prestigious Gold Award from International Design magazine's Design Review. Naylor has received numerous commissions including IBM, Crafts Council UK, Design Centre UK and Harrods.

Her research is concerned with the visual/cultural associations and implications of materials in the design process and outcome.

She has won several research awards, including most 5recently a major Arts and Humanities Innovation Research grant for 'Sustaining Desire: the chair as cultural, ecological and visual narrative; exploring the relationship between narrative, materiality and the emotive'.

Professor Naylor has taught at a number of highly distinguished universities in Europe and the United States. At the Royal College of Art she was Course Leader of Furniture in the School of Architecture and Design.

Professor Ralph Ball

Ralph Ball is Professor of Design at Central Saint Martins University of the Arts, London. Since graduating from the Royal College of Art in 1980 Ball has worked as a furniture and lighting designer with both critical and commercial success across the design field. His work has ranged from one-off commissions and interiors to mass produced design, winning Concord Illumination, British Design and Industries and IDSA design awards in Britain and the USA. His work is in permanent collections in the UK and USA, and he has exhibited work widely in the UK, Europe, Japan and the USA.

In the early 1980s, at Foster Associates , London, he designed furniture for the Renault Building in Swindon and for the Hong Kong and Shanghai Bank, Hong Kong. The widely acclaimed 'Renault Furniture' is the fore-runner of the Foster's 'Nomos' office system produced by Tecno SPA, Milan.

In 1988 he was appointed Professor of Industrial Design at the University of Washington USA, and has taught and lectured at many UK design colleges including the Royal College of Art.

He has completed two solo exhibitions in London: 'Modern Movements – Ralph Ball' at the Concord Sylvania Gallery, 1997, followed in 1998 by 'Ralph Ball – Introspective Furniture' at the Plateaux Gallery, Tower Bridge Piazza, London.

Studio Ball

In 2000, Maxine Naylor and Ralph Ball, together with Ralph's brother Keith Ball, set up studioball Art and Design. Studio partners work separately and in collaboration on a variety of installation, exhibition and individual projects. For further information, contact details and images of work from the studio visit the Studio Ball website: www.studioball.co.uk

Naylor and Ball currently design conceptual artifacts, which illuminate and question design culture. They call this activity 'Design Poetics'. Design Poetics forms an experimental, continuously evolving series of objects and collections, which act as commentaries and contemplations on the culture of Modernism, Postmodernism and contemporary design.

Black Dog Publishing
Architecture Art Design Fashion History
Photography Theory and Things

Designed by Emilia Gómez López

Black Dog Publishing Limited
Unit 4.4 Tea Building
56 Shoreditch High Street
London
E1 6JJ

Tel: +44 (0)20 7613 1922
Fax: +44 (0)20 7613 1944
Email: info@bdp.demon.co.uk
www.bdpworld.com

All opinions expressed within this publication are those of the
authors and not necessarily of the publisher.

British Library Cataloguing-in-Publication Data.

A catalogue record for this book is available from the British
Library.

ISBN 1 904772 21 8